The Classroom Manager

Procedures and Practices
to Improve Instruction

Suzanne G. Houff

ROWMAN & LITTLEFIELD EDUCATION
Lanham • Boulder • New York • Toronto • Plymouth, UK

Published in the United States of America
by Rowman & Littlefield Education
A Division of Rowman & Littlefield Publishers, Inc.
A wholly owned subsidary of The Rowman & Littlefield Publishing Group, Inc.
4501 Forbes Boulevard, Suite 200, Lanham, Maryland 20706
www.rowmaneducation.com

Estover Road
Plymouth PL6 7PY
United Kingdom

British Library Cataloguing in Publication Information Available

Library of Congress Cataloging-in-Publication Data

Houff, Suzanne G., 1953-
  The classroom manager : procedures and practices to improve instruction / Suzanne
G. Houff.
    p. cm.
  Includes bibliographical references.
  ISBN 978-1-57886-986-2 (cloth : alk. paper) — ISBN 978-1-57886-987-9 (pbk. : alk.
paper) — ISBN 978-1-57886-988-6 (electronic)
  1. Classroom management. I. Title.
  LB3013.H6616 2009
  371.102'4—dc22   2008047602

Printed in the United States of America

∞ ™ The paper used in this publication meets the minimum requirements of
American National Standard for Information Sciences—Permanence of Paper for
Printed Library Materials, ANSI/NISO Z39.48-1992.
Manufactured in the United States of America.

Contents

Introduction

This text is designed to introduce you to classroom management by providing a theoretical foundation and offering guidance in the development of a program that will work for you. Management focuses on student behaviors and the consequences of those behaviors. You will explore procedures and practices that help maintain harmony and improve classroom instruction.

By the time you complete this book and the outlined activities, you will be able to do the following:

- Demonstrate the needed knowledge, skills, and processes to support the learner through the practical application of theoretical approaches in classroom management skills
- Demonstrate an understanding of the diverse management approaches and theories based on student needs
- Develop a classroom community environment that promotes emotional well-being through effective management strategies and positive communication skills
- Develop and communicate classroom expectations that promote a safe learning environment and meet the needs of the learning community

Using William Glasser's (1986) ideas as a foundation, this text explores his five basic needs and their implication for classroom management. Additional research is enmeshed in the developmental recommendations so that you can provide theoretical and researched validation for your plan. Good intuition often guides educators in making the correct decisions, but without researched support, the decisions can be difficult to justify and trust.

By investigating Glasser's basic needs of survival, belonging, fun, freedom, and power, you will develop a management plan that will meet your classroom needs as well as those of your students.

As you work through this book, you will explore classroom management by first identifying your own beliefs regarding classroom behavior. Your needs and beliefs regarding student behavior may be different from another educator's beliefs. This is fine. Not all students learn the same, and not all educators teach in the same manner. The ultimate goal is to provide an environment conducive to student learning.

You will next look at learning theories and how they may impact your management style. Beliefs about learning provide a basis for diverse approaches to classroom management. This is followed by a study of Glasser's five basic needs. These needs are used as building blocks to look at areas of classroom management such as developing rules and procedures, ways to encourage appropriate behavior, and strategies for reducing inappropriate behaviors.

Part One

GETTING STARTED

You can't teach a man anything,
you can only help him find it within himself.

—Galileo

If there were one perfect way to maintain and manage a classroom, every teacher would immediately employ that strategy. Theory and research provide a good base on which to build beliefs, but sometimes theory can be confusing, overwhelming, and contradictory. Even as you dutifully post your rules and consequences for all to see, educational thinkers such as Alfie Kohn (1996) suggest that reward and punishment strategies do not work. You can't get Suzie to bring in her signed report card, but psychologist William Glasser (1986) suggests that Suzie needs to be empowered by giving her the responsibility for her own behavior.

Jane Nelson (1996) recommends that kindness, respect, and firmness are the ingredients needed for positive discipline, yet you know that Amad won't stop hitting the other students even if he does miss out on the surprise box filled with glorious treasures from the local dollar store. While the thinkers are thinking and writing their marvelous ideas, you are dealing with Raymond, who won't sit in his seat for anything less than a piece of candy.

You need a plan.

You will start this process of developing a management plan by first looking at how children learn.

Chapter One

What You Believe

You face difficult problems daily in the classroom. This text does not provide you with a smorgasbord of theoretical approaches to management theory but rather provides you with a format in which to develop an effective plan that is founded in research and theory.

For any education question, the best answer is, "It depends." This can be especially true when dealing with classroom management. Answers to your questions regarding the most effective way to manage a classroom depend on the situation, students, classroom factors, and your personal beliefs. I personally do not like the idea of giving food and candy as a reward to students for appropriate behavior. However, one year I had a particularly rowdy group that seemed to respond only to Jolly Ranchers. That year, I used Jolly Ranchers. I did what I needed to do to maintain some organization and sanity in order for learning to take place.

Before you begin this study of classroom management, take a moment to reflect on the classroom environment. What type of environment is comfortable for your teaching style? What are your needs in the classroom? Read the following questions and respond to these as a starting point in identifying your beliefs and developing your management program:

What do you see as the biggest problem in classroom management?

What do you consider a successful classroom?

Have you seen or used a successful management plan? What was it?

What made the plan successful?

Do you feel that you need to be in control of all situations in the classroom?

Describe your teaching style.

What are five questions you have regarding classroom management?

The management program that you develop for your classroom must fit your teaching style, personality, and beliefs. It should also be founded in quality research that offers direction and support for your practices. Most important, you need to remember that the reason for classroom management is to enhance learning for students.

What does research tell you about the classroom environment?

Read each of the following statements. Indicate whether you believe the statement is true or false:

_____1. Effective management skills come naturally.
_____2. Direct teaching of rules and procedures should begin in elementary school.
_____3. It is important to demand obedience in order to maintain classroom order.
_____4. We may be squelching any motivation to learn and behave if we offer rewards as a motivation.
_____5. Emotional intelligence cannot be taught or strengthened.
_____6. Studies indicate that the use of praise as your management plan will cause disruptive behavior to cease.
_____7. Reprimands that are delivered loudly and publicly are more effective in stopping disruptive behavior than reprimands that are given quietly and calmly.

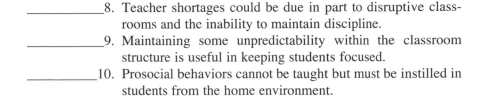

          8. Teacher shortages could be due in part to disruptive classrooms and the inability to maintain discipline.

          9. Maintaining some unpredictability within the classroom structure is useful in keeping students focused.

          10. Prosocial behaviors cannot be taught but must be instilled in students from the home environment.

How did you do?

1. False: According to Marzano, Marzano, and Pickering (2003) and Marzano (2003), classroom management skills can be learned.
2. True: According to Woolfolk (2008), the direct teaching of rules and procedures is vital in elementary school.
3. False: According to Marzano, Marzano, and Pickering (2003), the current shift in the field is moving from demanding obedience to teaching self-control.
4. True: According to Kohn (1993), "We may kill off interest in the very thing we are bribing them to do" (p. 72).
5. False: According to Norris (2003), unlike IQ, emotional intelligence can be taught. Students can acquire the skill to become aware of their own emotions and the emotions of others.
6. False: McGoey and DePaul (2000) found that using praise or positive consequences as the only management strategy would not cause disruptive behavior to stop.
7. False: Landrum and Kauffman (2006) found the opposite to be true.
8. True: Ingersoll and Smith (2003) found that disruptive behavior led teachers to leave the field.
9. False: Oliver and Reschly (2007) suggest that in unpredictable situations, students will behave in a manner to create predictability even in cases where negative consequences are predictable.
10. False: Turnbull et al. (2002) found that schoolwide teaching of prosocial behavior showed a significant reduction in discipline problems.

Using your responses to the management questions and the true-or-false statements, summarize your beliefs or your philosophy regarding classroom management in the following space:

Chapter Two

Learning to Change Behavior

If you were to do extensive research in the field of classroom management, you would find that there are numerous approaches and theories. As illustrated in the true-or-false statements, many times those approaches and theories are contradictory. Ultimately, the program must meet your needs as well as the student needs. Your knowledge about how a child learns is a good place for you to begin in the development of an effective classroom program.

BEHAVIORAL THEORY

Behavioral approaches to learning offer an explanation of learning that focuses on the external events that cause a change in behavior. These theorists suggest that when learning takes place, it can be observed through the behavior or actions of the learner. A change of behavior can be observed. Behaviorists believe that students take a passive role in learning by simply responding to a stimulus. For example, each time Don Jr. brings in his homework on time, the teacher places a smiley sticker on his daily agenda to go home. Don Jr. learns to associate his homework (response) to a smiley sticker (stimulus).

Teachers who use external rewards and consequences to alter classroom behavior subscribe to the behavioral approach of learning and behavior modification beliefs of discipline. They use outside reinforcers to try to bring about a change in behavior. A reinforcer is any consequence that follows and strengthens a behavior. Reinforcers can be positive or negative.

Take the example of Don Jr. and the homework. The smiley sticker is a positive reinforcer if Don Jr. likes the smiley faces and wants to continue to earn them. The behavior, turning in homework, is strengthened by a desired stimulus, the smiley face. A negative reinforcement takes place when a behavior is strengthened by the removal of an unpleasant stimulus. Let's say that Don Jr. knew that if he did not bring in his homework, he would automatically receive half an hour of lunch detention. He brings in his homework, and the threat of detention is removed, and he has therefore been negatively reinforced.

Negative reinforcement is not punishment. Both positive and negative reinforcement strengthen a behavior. Punishment is given to try to stop or reduce the behavior. If Don Jr. does not bring in his homework and has to stay for detention, he is receiving punishment. Studies by behaviorist B. F. Skinner and subsequent studies regarding punishment suggest that people are more motivated to learn and behave when rewards rather than punishments are used.

"Behavior modification" is a term used when applying behavioral learning theory to changing behavior. Behavior modification can be implemented in the classroom by addressing the following three questions: what behavior needs to be changed, what interventions will be put into place to change the behavior, and how will the results be tracked?

First, clearly identify and define the behavior that needs to be changed in the students or student. What specifically needs to be altered? What actions are you going to take prior to the behavior (antecedents) or after the behavior (consequences) to intervene? How are you going to keep track of the behavior to know if your plan is working?

Let's return to Don Jr. and his homework. Don Jr. has trouble bringing in his homework. You realize that this behavior needs to be changed. Don Jr. needs to bring his homework in daily, so you tell him that for every day he brings in his homework, you will place a smiley sticker on his paper to go home. In order to know if the intervention is working, you need to keep track of how many days Don Jr. brings in his homework and receives a smiley face.

Read the following classroom scenario. How would a behaviorist suggest that you respond to the situation?

Lamont and Ryan are the class clowns. They are always trying to get attention through their classroom antics and comments. Lately, they have found much fun in making bodily function noises. The rest of the class usually laughs, and some have started to mimic the sounds. You have already spoken to them once. Each student has gotten their name written on the board. Now what?

Using the previous scenario, address each of the following questions:

How could positive reinforcement be used to change the behavior of the boys?

How could negative reinforcement be used to change the behavior of the boys?

How could punishment be used to change the behavior of the boys?

COGNITIVE THEORY

Cognitive theorists suggest that learning requires active participation for students to process information. Students are not a blank slate on which knowledge is written; rather, behavior changes as a result of cognitive processing or thinking. Learning takes place through accommodating knowledge in a new schemata or assimilating new knowledge in a schemata that is already in place.

The schemata can be thought of as a metaphorical file cabinet of the mind. New information is filed in a preexisting folder, or, if there is no preexisting folder, a new folder is made for the information. If the information is not accommodated or assimilated, that is, if the information is not filed away, it is lost.

For example, you are presenting a new story titled "Suzie Going to the Sea" to a second-grade reading group. What if the group of second graders lives in Kansas and has never seen the sea? They have no folder in which to place the information contained in the story. They cannot comprehend the elements or visualize what they read unless they have some prior knowledge with which to relate the information. You must develop a "sea file folder" or schemata for your students. Show pictures, play sound tapes, spray ocean breeze air freshener, get sand, and provide anything else that will help the students conceptualize the sea.

Cognitive learning theory applied to behavior management implies that students must have a "file folder" for a desired behavior and an understanding of the reason for the behavior. Let's say that one of your rules is to "share." Unless the students understand sharing, they cannot practice it. Therefore, you must offer illustrations of what sharing looks like and how it is done. Students can then develop an understanding of why the rule is important and work through the processes of maintaining the rule. Cognitive behavior management (CBM) is one approach in using the cognitive learning theory.

CBM uses cognitive learning to focus on the student as an active learner in changing his or her behavior. Rather than teaching the fact that a certain behavior will result in a reward or consequence, the focus is on teaching a behavior skill. The teacher models an appropriate behavior skill that the student observes and then practices.

Through the use of critical-thinking and problem-solving skills, the student gradually takes over the responsibility of monitoring and evaluating his or her own behavior. This shift in focus from the teacher to the student allows the student to function independently and interdependently in the classroom community. It is hoped that students can generalize the behavior to other learning situations. Meichenbaum (cited in Woolfolk, 2008) proposes the following steps for CBM implementation:

Teacher models the task or behavior using a think-aloud or self-talk format.
Student performs the task under guided practice.
Student performs the task using a think-aloud or self-talk format.
Student performs the task while mentally working through the process.

Read the following scenario. How would a cognitivist suggest that you manage the situation? What could be used to help motivate Clay to complete his work?

Clay has recently slacked off in his work. He has been turning in assignments late and incomplete. The bad grades do not seem to make a difference to him. Just today, he came and told you he did not have his social studies project that was due today. He wants to turn it in tomorrow.

AFFECTIVE THEORY

The affective approach to learning focuses on motivation and attitude. Both cognitive and behavior theories have a bidirectional relationship with affective learning since motivation and attitude affect thinking and behavior, while thinking and behavior affect motivation and attitude.

Motivation and attitude can be thought of as mental processes that direct actions. To determine the learning motivation of your students, consider the following questions:

What motivates the student to learn?
What determines the readiness or willingness to learn?
How dedicated is the student to the learning process?
What will decide the determination or intensity of the learning?
How does the learning engagement make the student feel? (Woolfolk, 2008)

If these questions are significant and applicable in the learning process, they will be relevant to the changing behavior process as well. When applying these questions to behavior, you might ask yourself, What motivates the student to behave in a certain manner? What determines if the student is ready and willing to change a behavior? Is the student dedicated to the process? What will determine if the student will remain motivated to change? How does the new behavior affect the student's feelings? By looking into the emotional processes of the students, you can tap into their intrinsic or extrinsic motivations to affect behavior.

An extrinsically motivated student will respond to external rewards and punishments such as candy, extra free time, detention, and so on. The intrinsically motivated student seeks internal reward and self-satisfaction. The knowledge of motivation type can help you identify the best method to use with the student.

Affective management behaviors center on developing the motivation and attitude to change behaviors through the process of identifying new behaviors, differentiating the new behaviors from the old, and integrating the new behaviors to self.

Read the following scenario. How would an affective theorist suggest that you manage the situation?

Buzzy is very good natured and easy to get along with as long as he has no demands placed on him. When given restrictions or requirements, he becomes very defiant. Getting him to turn in work is impossible. He will not do homework or classwork but prefers to be left alone in the back of the room. Yesterday you noticed that he was taking his desk apart. There were screws and bolts surrounding his desk.

SOCIAL THEORY

The social learning model provides a link between the behavior and cognitive models in that the theory suggests that learning takes place through the observation and imitation of others. Social theorist Albert Bandura (1977, 1986) believes that social and environmental interactions affect learning. He expands the behaviorist learning view to include observation.

For observational learning to take place, Bandura suggests that four elements be in place. First, the student must be paying attention. If you do not have the student's attention, observation will not take place. Second, the student needs to remember what was observed. Retention can be improved through implementing strategies of visualization, or rehearsal. Next, the student needs an opportunity to practice the new learning. Finally, motivation comes into play. If the student is not motivated to learn, the learning will not take place.

Bandura's steps applied to behavior management suggest that you need to first capture the student's attention. Having gained the student's attention puts a significant responsibility on you that cannot be taken lightly. You are a model for the behavior you would like to see in your classroom. Students watch what you do and how you interact with others. Be careful with your body language and your tone. Remain aware of and respect the amount of influence that you have on your students.

Once you have gained their attention, help develop the students' mental schemata so that they can visualize and maintain the behavior. Provide planned situations for students to practice the new behaviors. Catch them at demonstrating appropriate behaviors and validate their attempts in unplanned situations. Use a "caught-being-good" approach where rewards or incentives are given when you witness an exceptional behavior. The Internet is full of sites that offer coupons, certificates, and buttons that can be awarded. This approach can be implemented on the individual or the group level.

Each time a student or group receives a "caught being good," he or she receives a token toward earning a larger goal. For example, each time an individual student is "caught," he may have his name placed in a box. At the end of the week or month, a name is drawn from the box to receive a reward. The more times a student is "caught," the more chances he has of earning the reward. The same idea works on the group level. Each time the group or class is "caught," they may receive a marble in a jar. When the jar is full, they earn a class reward.

These rewards or incentives can improve the climate of the classroom by building camaraderie in working toward a common goal. They can also take different forms. Incentives or rewards may come in the form of recognition, special events, or tangible items. Perhaps the class might work together to earn a pizza party at the end of the month or a week without homework. The individual student might work toward recognition on a bulletin board or 10 minutes of free time.

According to Bandura's design, you need to offer this reinforcement to enhance motivation. The goal is for the student to learn how to perform the behavior and realize the outcome of the behavior.

A social approach to management focuses on the interdependent relationships within the classroom. Students react and interact to the social element of the group. Change in behavior is affected by the environment, the individual, or the behavior and the interaction of these elements.

Read the following classroom scenario. How would a social theorist suggest that you respond to the situation?

> During the literature circle, Jamie and Fiona talk about everything except the novel they are reading. You have assigned each of them a job within the group so that they would each be held accountable for some work. They complete the work minimally and continue to carry on the conversation. Other members of the group are becoming irritated and resentful.

ECOLOGICAL THEORY

Bronfenbrenner's (1997) ecological systems theory expands Bandura's view of the role environment plays in the development and learning of the child. He proposes that the child develops in a complex structure of interrelating relationships. Environment and biological factors work together to shape and change the child. Relationships are bidirectional, meaning that the child is shaped by those around him or her and that those around him or her are influenced by the child.

Bronfenbrenner (1997) outlines five influential environmental learning systems: microsystem, mesosystem, exosystem, macrosystem, and chronosystem. Visualize this system as an onion and its layers. The very core of the onion is the microsystem. This core focuses on the relationship between the student and his or her immediate environment or surroundings, such as family/caregiver, school, peers, and community.

The next layer or mesosystem builds on the earlier interaction by looking at two microsystems and the connection between them. One microsystem is the student and the home, while another microsystem is the student and the school. A mesosystem is the interaction of home and school. The next layer is referred to as the exosystem. This layer includes the environment that indirectly affects the development of the student. Examples include extended family, friends of the family, media, or caregiver workplace.

The macrosystem, or next layer, deals with the influence of cultural context. Cultural patterns and beliefs regarding religion, politics, and ethnicity shape the development of the student. The outer layer of the onion is the chronosystem, or patterns and transitions through life (Figure 2.1).

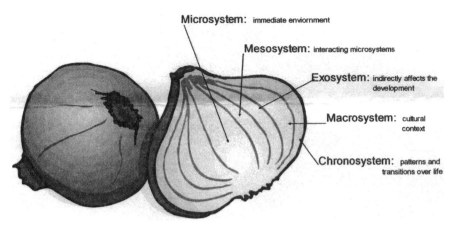

Figure 2.1. Bronfenbrenner's environmental system

Bronfenbrenner's interactive layers are relevant for classroom behavior in that they provide a rationale for some of the beliefs and behaviors you may encounter in the classroom. Just as schemata play a role in learning, they also play a role in the prior knowledge a student brings into the classroom. Before the student came into your classroom, he or she was influenced by ecological factors that helped develop the behavior and attitude.

Bronfenbrenner's ecological layers in learning will not necessarily provide you with a foundation on which to build a management theory but will, it is hoped, provide you with information and ideas that will lead you into the development of an accepting and understanding classroom climate.

Read the following scenario. How would an ecological theorist respond to the situation?

> Darlene knows that chewing gum is not allowed in school. Yet, as you turn back from the blackboard, you notice that she puts a piece of bubblegum in her mouth. So as not to disturb the lesson, you choose to ignore the infraction for now. When she catches your eye, she blows a big pink bubble.

These theories are not self-contained in scope but are overlapping in practice as illustrated in Figure 2.2.

Complete Table 2.1 by describing how each of these learning theories would be implemented in classroom management practices. For example, the behavioral approach to management would include some type of negative or positive reinforcer immediately after a behavior to increase the likelihood that the behavior will be repeated. When Jermaine brings in his homework, you might positively reinforce that behavior by giving him a star on his chart.

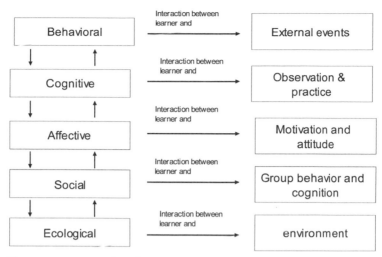

Figure 2.2. Interaction chart

When Shirley completes her work and sits quietly reading a book, you might negatively reinforce that behavior by taking away her homework assignment for the evening.

After you have completed the table, look back at your philosophy that you started in the beginning of this chapter. How would you revise your statements based on learning theory covered in this chapter?

Table 2.1. Classroom Implementation

Theory	Classroom Implementation
Behavioral	
Cognitive	
Affective	
Social	
Ecological	

SUMMARY

- Learning is a process that impacts how students act, think, and feel.
- If you want your students to learn and practice new behavior, you must first identify your beliefs concerning how children learn.
- Learning theories are statements and principles based on observation and research that attempt to explain how learning takes place.
- Theories discussed in this chapter include the following:

Behavior
Cognitive
Affective
Social
Ecological

- The behavioral theory views learning through stimulus and response.
- Cognitive theory is student centered with an active approach to learning.
- The affective approach places consideration in motivation and attitude in learning and classroom management.
- Social theory suggests that students learn from observation and interaction with others.
- The ecological theory of learning explores the experiences and beliefs a student brings to the classroom as a result of his or her environment.
- Learning takes place as the result of not one action or theory but rather a combination of interacting factors.

ON YOUR OWN

Reread your own philosophy on learning. Are your ideas grounded more in one theory than another? Why? Does one theory play a less significant role in your philosophy than the other theories? Why?

FURTHER READING

Elementary Focus

Charles, C. M. (2000). *The synergetic classroom: Joyful teaching and gentle discipline*. New York: Longman.

DiGennaro, F., Martens, B. K., & McIntyre, L. L. (2005). Increasing treatment integrity through negative reinforcement: Effects on teacher and student behavior. *School Psychology Review, 34*(2), 220–231.

Elias, M., et al. (1997). How to launch a social and emotional learning program. *Educational Leadership, 54*(8), 15–19.

Hofer, M. (2007). Goal conflicts and self-regulation: A new look at pupils' off-task behavior in the classroom. *Educational Research Review, 2*(1), 28–38.

Johnson, D. W., & Johnson, R. T. (1999). The three Cs of school and classroom management. In H. J. Freiberg (Ed.), *Beyond behaviorism: Changing the classroom management paradigm* (pp. 119–144). Boston: Allyn & Bacon.

Norris, J. G. (2003). Looking at classroom management through social and emotional learning lens. *Theory Into Practice, 42*(4), 313–318.

Secondary Focus

Cameron, J. (2001) Negative effects of reward on intrinsic motivation—A limited phenomenon: Comment on Deci, Koestner, and Ryan (2001). *Review of Educational Research, 71*(1), 29–42.

Doyle, W. (2006). Ecological approaches to classroom management. In C. M. Evertson & C. S. Weinstein (Eds.), *Handbook of classroom management: Research, practice and contemporary issues* (pp. 97–125). Mahwah, NJ: Lawrence Erlbaum Associates.

Instrator, S. M. (2003). Tuned in and fired up: *How teaching can inspire real learning in the classroom.* New Haven, CT: Yale University Press.

Gable, R. A., Hester, P., & Hester, L. (2005). Cognitive, affective, and relational dimensions of middle school students: Implications for improving discipline and instruction. *The Clearing House, 79*(1), 40–44.

Roeser, R. W., Eccles, J. S., & Sameroff, A. J. (2000). School as a context of early adolescents' academic and social-emotional development: A summary of research findings. *Elementary School Journal, 100*(5), 443–471.

Ryan, A., & Patrick, H. (2001). The classroom social environment and changes in adolescents' motivation and engagement during middle school. *American Educational Research Journal, 38*(2), 437–460.

Part Two

MEETING STUDENT NEEDS

As long as it's important for adults to win,
they are making losers out of children.

—Jane Nelson

William Glasser (1986, 1993) suggests that when students misbehave, they are trying to tell you something and that, according to his theories, one or more of their needs for survival, belonging, fun, freedom, or power is not being met.

Building on his basic needs and control theory, he published *Choice Theory* in 1999. In this text, he postulates that each person chooses his or her behavior on the basis of his or her drive to satisfy a basic need. Using his theory as a basis for classroom management, you can enhance the student's intrinsic motivation by meeting his or her needs and allowing him or her to make choices. Rather than demanding work and appropriate behavior from students, Glasser's ideas offer strategies to motivate students in making choices that will help them successfully fit in the world around them and reach their goals.

In the 1970s, Abraham Maslow put forth a hierarchy of motivation levels. These levels, also based on needs, include physiological needs, security, love and belonging, esteem, and self-actualization. Physiological needs deal with survival, including food, drink, and shelter. Maslow believed that these needs must be met first before any of the other needs or levels could be met and that there was a linear progression through the levels. One level must be met before moving on to the next.

The security level in Maslow's hierarchy goes beyond the physical domain and focuses more on the emotional sense of security and safety within family and society. Also dealing with the emotional domain is the level of belonging and love. This level includes elements of giving and receiving love and

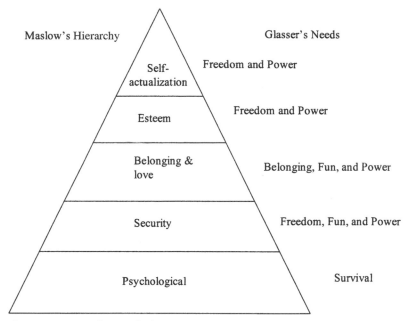

Figure P2.1. Maslow and Glasser

friendship. Esteem, as a motivational level, focuses on the respect of self and others. He suggests that people are motivated by achievement and that through this achievement they acquire confidence. Very few people reach the highest level of self-actualization, or the complete acceptance of self. It is at this level that a complete understanding and fulfillment of self is reached.

Glasser, although similar in thought to Maslow, does not suggest a hierarchy but instead believes that each individual simultaneously experiences needs and fulfills those needs at an individual level. Both believe that actions are reflective of how well the needs are being met. Figure P2.1 illustrates the overlapping and correlation of their ideas.

The ideas of basic needs and motivation are introduced here to illustrate the overlapping and interdependent relationships of motivation, basic needs, and management. The correlation of Maslow's motivation hierarchy and Glasser's basic needs provides a basis to develop a management program in which the student's needs are being met and the motivation to make good choices is enhanced.

This part of the text explores each of Glasser's needs in terms of meaning and classroom application. Each chapter begins with a scenario for analysis. This is followed by a word organizer that provides guidance in the development of a definition, examples, nonexamples, and a classroom application of the need. Each term is then explored through classroom examples and exercises.

Chapter Three

Survival

SITUATION

Essie's uniform is tattered, wrinkled, and basically dirty. The other students in class make fun of her. She is currently living with her grandmother since the whereabouts of her parents are unknown. It is assumed they are on the streets. The last time anyone heard from her mother, she was prostituting for drug money.

During computer time, you found out that some of the girls laughingly showed Essie where a site had been created on a Web page that included a picture of her in the locker room. In addition, there were some cruel comments and vicious statements about her.

Although Essie did not approach you about the incident, you feel like something needs to be done. This behavior outside the classroom is affecting the work that is going on in the classroom.

Situation Analysis

What is the problem in Essie's situation? Do you think she feels safe in her environment? Why? How would this affect her learning? Is there anything you can do? (Figure 3.1).

Survival suggests that students have the physiological needs to live or to get through life. This includes nourishment, shelter, and safety. It does not mean technology, cars, toys, video games, and cell phones, although your students may disagree. In the classroom, survival might look like students who have been fed, have slept, and are comfortable and secure in a safe environment.

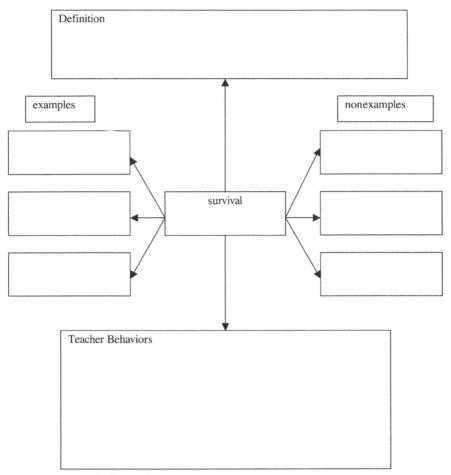

Figure 3.1.　Survival organizer

NOURISHMENT

The idea that there is a link between nutrition and brain function is not new. Both qualitative and quantitative studies have looked closely at how a proper diet affects the thought process. Studies completed by the American School Food Service Association (1989) indicate a correlation between low protein intake and low achievement scores. Additional studies show a link between breakfast and brain function.

Students who have breakfast continually perform better than children who have not had breakfast. Because of the vast amount of research based on nutrition and learning, schools have put into place several initiatives to try to ensure that students come to the classroom well fed and ready to learn.

In 2006, the National School lunch program federally assisted 101,000 public and nonprofit private schools. Thirty million students were served a reduced or free lunch. At the same time, 84,000 schools received federal assistance for school breakfast. Not only do the students score better on the standardized test scores, but they are better behaved and are less hyperactive than students who have skipped breakfast.

SHELTER

Homelessness affects every aspect of a child's development. Homeless children enter schools with physical, psychological, and emotional issues that put them at a huge disadvantage for experiencing success in the classroom. Studies indicate that they not only consistently score in the lowest percentile on achievement tests but also are more frequently diagnosed with mental disorders than their sheltered classmates. Homeless students need additional health and learning services yet ironically may have limited access to these services because of their homelessness.

The number of homeless children in schools is difficult to count. Currently, two types of methods are used to keep track of the homeless population. These include point-in-time and period prevalence. The point-in-time method counts all people who are homeless on a given day or given week. Period prevalence counts the number of homeless over a given period of time.

MSNBC (2005) reports that 74,000 people were homeless in 2005. The National Coalition for Homeless reports that in 2000 there were 1.35 million children in the United States who were homeless on any given night. In 2003, children under the age of 18 accounted for 39% of the homeless population, and 49% of that population were under the age of five. Single women with children make up the fastest-growing population of homeless.

These discouraging statistics have strong implications for student's classroom success. Although you may not be able to consistently and directly impact food and shelter for a student, you have the primary influence and responsibility in developing a safe classroom environment.

SAFETY

I will never forget the time that Gary did not bring in his homework. Gary was usually a student who strived to do well and keep up with his work until this one particular day when he sat looking guilty, dumbfounded, and tired. I must not have had too much coffee that morning because I handled the situation calmly and privately. Gary and I talked about the missing work, and through teary eyes he explained to me that both his parents had been drunk the night before. Their drunkenness led to an argument that ended when the police showed up to take dad to jail. It seems that Gary spent the night at the jail waiting with mom for the bail money. Homework was not the biggest concern in this child's life. He hadn't slept or eaten. His safety and environment were being threatened.

There is not a great deal you can do in this type of situation other than contacting social services and the counselor. However, you can make the classroom a safe environment that is free of threats from other students and threats of humiliation and failure. You might provide the only consistency and safety the student experiences. Safety comes from the classroom's structure, predictability, and consistency as a result of established rules and procedures.

Safety Through Rules and Procedures

On the very first day of class, have a basic idea of what rules you want in the class and use your ideas to guide students in the establishment of rules. Give students ownership in deciding the three to five basic rules that keep the classroom a safe environment. Keep the rules stated in positive terms. For example, one rule might state that everyone needs to show respect. This very generic rule covers a multitude of behaviors, from fighting to rudeness. Rather than stating the rule as "no disrespect," the rule can be stated as "show respect toward everyone." As students develop the rule, allow them to discuss the meaning.

Let them describe what the rule might look like in the classroom and what it does not look like. Encourage the students to give specific examples of the rule in and out of class. They might cut out pictures to illustrate or role-play situations that demonstrate the ideal behind the rule. Allow them the opportunity to visualize and experience the abstract idea. It is through this teaching and modeling that students gain a true understanding of what the rule is and why the rule is important. The word organizers at the beginning of each section provide an excellent format to follow. These organizers help students take the abstract rule and make it a concrete action.

You might even develop a student contract or document that outlines the rules students have developed. You, the students, and the caregivers sign the contract so that everyone is aware of the classroom expectations. Hold onto these documents—they might come in handy at some point in the school year.

What three to five rules do you think are needed in your classroom? Write those rules here:

For each of the rules you listed, use Table 3.1 to provide a description of how that rule would look in the classroom. How could you teach the rule?
Useful websites for developing classroom rules include the following:

http://www.educationworld.com/a_lesson/lesson/lesson274.shtml
http://www.plsweb.com/resources/newsletters/enews_archives/32/2003/
    09/01
http://www.laruekerr.com/classroomrulesprocedures.htm
http://www.proteacher.org/c/188_Classroom_Procedures.html
http://www.canteach.ca/elementary/classman1.html
http://www.windsor.k12.co.us/skyview/cduran/Rules%20and%20Routines
    .htm
http://www.teachersnetwork.org/ntol/howto/manage/c13801.htm
http://content.scholastic.com/browse/article.jsp?id=3608

Procedures or routines offer a way to maintain order and safety in the classroom. Although procedure and routine development and instruction can

Table 3.1. Rule chart

Rule	How It Looks	How It Is Taught

Figure 3.2. Management signs

be time consuming since preplanning and organization are necessary, they can create a manageable and organized structure. Procedures result in less teacher talk.

Classroom signs also help in reducing teacher talk. Rather than flipping the lights or raising your voice to get attention, you can hold up a sign. Instead of telling students to clear their desks, hold up a sign that states, "Clear your desks." You could even appoint an official sign holder as a weekly classroom job. Make the signs large enough to see and colorful enough to get attention (Figure 3.2).

Complete the teacher procedure chart to brainstorm some classroom procedures you could have in place in your classroom (Figure 3.3). Procedure ideas might include taking attendance, checking homework, and taking lunch count. For example, you might want to write each student's name on a clothespin. As the student enters the class in the morning, he or she takes his clothespin and clips it to a poster indicating the type of lunch he or she will have that day. You have managed to get the attendance and the lunch count. What other routines or procedures can you think of? (Figure 3.3).

Look back at your list. Which of those can be performed by the student without disruption to you? What conditions need to be set? What guidelines need to be in place?

What will the teacher do to:

Assign and collect homework?	
Pick class helpers?	
Distribute materials?	
Take attendance?	
Take lunch count?	
Contact parents?	
Help a student that has been absent?	
Get the class's attention?	
Other:	
Other:	

Figure 3.3. Teacher procedure chart

For example, what if the student needs to sharpen a pencil? It would behoove you to have a basket of sharpened pencil nubs. The pencil nubs are those little bits of pencils that are found on the classroom floor at the end of the day. They usually are without an eraser and have a few unidentified teeth marks in them. If a student breaks a pencil, have them exchange their broken one for a sharpened nub. At the end of the day or at a pencil sharpening break, they may exchange their pencils back.

This routine puts a stop to pencil sharpener traffic. Going to the pencil sharpener can be an exciting event if the student is unengaged or not interested in the lesson. Trips to the pencil sharpener offer opportunities to kick another student, pass a note, or just cause a distraction, if needed. The nub basket routine can offer a win–win situation, especially if you purchase an electric pencil sharpener and use sharpening nubs as a reward at the end of the day.

Complete the student procedure chart in Figure 3.4 to brainstorm some classroom events for which you might need an established routine. Ideas

What will the students do:

When they first enter the classroom?	
When they need to go to the bathroom?	
When they need to sharpen their pencils?	
When they leave at the end of the day?	
When they move through the halls?	
When all their seatwork is completed?	
When they need the teacher?	
Other:	
Other:	

Figure 3.4.   Student procedure chart

could include going to the bathroom, sharpening pencils, or turning in homework. What other routines or procedures can you think of?

The following website will provide you with additional ideas:

http://www.nea.org/classmanagement/proced040826.html

BULLYING

In the past few years, bullying has received a great deal of attention. More recently, cyberbullying has become the focus of bullies and bullying. Cyberbullying consists of intentional and repeated verbal slanders or threats through electronic devices, such as e-mail, instant messaging, or personal Web pages. Personal information and pictures are posted without the consent of the owner, and in some cases the bully assumes the other person's identity for purposes of humiliation or defamation.

The following story is a common occurrence. In retaliation for a slight shown to her daughter, a neighborhood mother took on the identity of a young man interested in a young girl named Kelly. Through an online chat room, the mother led Kelly to believe that this young man was enamored with her and wanted a relationship. When he unexpectedly broke up with her by writing belittling and hurtful comments, the distraught Kelly killed herself.

The following is based on a 2004 survey of 1,500 students conducted by i-SAFE (found in Hitchcock, 2007):

- 42% of students have been bullied online. One in four have had it happen more than once.
- 35% have been threatened online. Nearly one in five have had it happen more than once.
- 21% have received mean or threatening e-mails or other messages.
- 58% admit someone has said mean or hurtful things to them online.
- 53% admit to having said something mean or hurtful to another person online. More than one in three has done it more than once.
- 58% have not told their parents or an adult about something mean or hurtful that happened to them online.

These are frightening statistics, and even though blocks and filters may reduce this threat on school computers, the act and the ramifications have a drastic impact on the school environment. If your school does not have a rule and policy on cyberbullying, take charge in bringing about a change to develop the rule and policy. Make sure that all involved stakeholders are

educated about cyberbullying and the actions and consequences that occur if
the act is discovered. If threats occur, take the immediate action prescribed by
your school policy. Students need to be aware that cyberbullying constitutes
a computer crime and is punishable by law.

Useful websites for cyberbullying include the following:

http://www.stopcyberbullying.org
http://en.wikipedia.org/wiki/Cyber-bullying
http://www.ala.org/ala/washoff/woissues/techinttele/internetsafety/internet-
    safety.cfm

SUMMARY

- You cannot expect students to learn if they do not feel safe and secure in
  their environment. Although you cannot have much control over their eat-
  ing and sleeping habits, you can remember that these issues play a role in
  how the student performs and acts in class.
- Established rules and procedures bring consistency and control to the classroom that bring about a feeling of structure and safety.
- Start the year with three to five rules in mind but allow students to help
  develop those rules.
- Rules and procedures need to be taught.
- The Internet introduces a new threat to safety and a new venue for bullying.

ON YOUR OWN

In what type of environment do you feel the safest? Describe the lighting,
temperature, and surroundings. Does the environment that you describe offer
physical or psychological safety? How?

FURTHER READING

Elementary Focus

Beane, A. L. (1999). *The bully free classroom: Over 100 tips and strategies for teach-
    ers K–8*. Minneapolis: Free Spirit.
Bohn, C. M., Roehrig, A. D., & Pressley, M. (2004). The first days of school in the
    classrooms of two more effective and four less effective primary-grade teachers.
    Elementary School Journal, 104(4), 269–287.

Brady, K., Forton, M. B., Porter, D., & Wood, C. (2003). *Rules in school.* Greenfield, MA: Northeast Foundation for Children.

Bucher, K. T., & Manning, L. (2005). Creating safe schools. *The Clearing House, 79*(1), 55–60.

Froschl, M., & Gropper, N. (1999). Fostering friendships, curbing bullying. *Educational Leadership, 56*(8), 72–75.

Lundeberg, M. A., Emmett, J., Osland, P. A., & Lindquist, N. (1997). Down with put-downs! *Educational Leadership, 55*(2), 36–37.

Secondary Focus

Barton, P. E., Coley, R. J., & Wenglinsky, H. (1998). *Order in the classroom: Violence, discipline, and student achievement.* Princeton, NJ: Educational Testing Service.

Bichard, D. F. (2000). Using classroom rules to construct behavior. *Middle School Journal, 31*(5), 37–45.

Espelage, D. K., & Swearer, S. M. (Eds.). *Bullying in American schools: A social-ecological perspective on prevention and intervention.* Mahwah, NJ: Lawrence Erlbaum Associates.

Howell, J. C., & Lynch, J. P. (2000). *Youth gangs in schools.* Washington, DC: Office of Juvenile Justice and Delinquency Prevention, U.S. Department of Justice. Available: http://www.ncjrs.org/html/ojjdp/jjbul2000_8_2/contents.html

Langford, P. E., Lovegrove, H., & Lovegrove, M. (1994). Do senior secondary students possess the moral maturity to negotiate class rules? *Journal of Moral Education, 23*(4), 387–407.

Richard, A. (1999, September 8). As students return, focus in on security. *Education Week, 1,* 12–15.

Schmollinger, C. S., Opaleski, K., Chapman, M. L., Jocius, R., & Bell, S. (2002). How do you make your classroom an inviting place for students to come back to each year? *English Journal, 91*(6), 20–22.

Wessler, S. L. (2003). It's hard to learn when you're scared. *Educational Leadership, 61*(1), 40–42.

Chapter Four

Belonging

SITUATION

It is already November, and I just had a new student placed in my class. He moved here from someplace in the Middle East, and I don't have any records for him. His English is okay, but I can't really tell which reading group to put him in. Plus, he doesn't seem to get along with any of my other fourth-grade students. He dresses and speaks differently from all the others. Just the other day, he started a fight at recess, and I had to send him to the office. I don't understand why these people can't just wait until the beginning of the next school year to enroll him. I was not at all pleased when the assistant principal brought him to my class in the middle of my lesson on verbs. I had to stop right in the middle of class and get him situated with a seat, books, and materials to take home that afternoon.

Situation Analysis

What is the problem in the situation? Do you think the issue is that the student has entered the classroom after school has been in session for several months? Probably not. The issue here is the teacher. Why? What should have been done in this situation? (Figure 4.1).

Belonging means to feel comfortable and accepted as a part of a group or community. It means feeling valued as a member of that group and making contributions to the whole. Belonging is demonstrated through a show of respect between you, the student, and all class members. This feeling of belonging comes about as a result of the efforts you make in establishing a positive classroom environment.

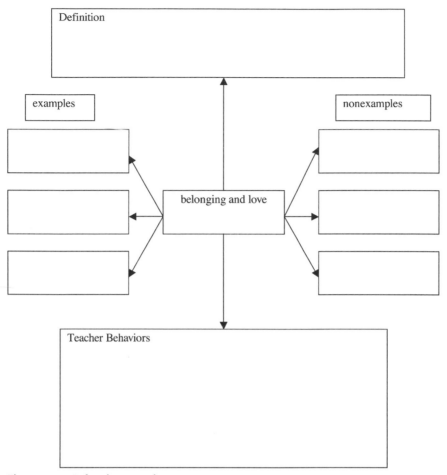

Figure 4.1. Belonging organizer

A positive classroom climate is one in which everyone is acknowledged and valued. There is no criticism, sarcasm, or exclusion. You know each student's background and educational needs. You and the class work to develop a community climate that is conducive to learning. Active listening is practiced.

Active listening is a way of focusing on the speaker and what the speaker is saying in order to provide a response that enhances a mutual understanding. Rather than thinking of how to respond to the person talking, the listener focuses on what the speaker is actually saying. The listener can then respond by paraphrasing or repeating what the speaker has said in order to clear up any miscommunication.

How can you develop a classroom community? Why should you bother? Research supports the idea that children's academic achievement is increased in a safe, nurturing, and affirming environment (Elias et al., 1997). This safe, nurturing, and affirming environment does not just happen but has to be developed and modeled through classroom instruction. In this chapter, you will look at ways to establish a community of learners through knowing your students, developing cooperation, and implementing class meetings.

KNOWING YOUR STUDENTS

How can you get to know your students? You might start by looking in their cumulative folder. The information can provide some idea of their background and the knowledge base they bring to your classroom. You could also talk to other teachers, but be very careful in this situation. Your perceptions may be entirely different from those of previous teachers, and it would be a shame to prejudice your attitude and feelings before ever meeting the child.

Surveys provide a means to gather useful information. You can find out a great deal of information by asking the right questions. You might want to know what the student's favorite television show is. The answer could tell you how late the child is staying up, what interests him, and the level of supervision on his or her viewing. What are five insightful questions you would include on a survey? What do you think is important to know about your students? How would you use this information? Use the chart in Table 4.1 to start brainstorming types of information you want to gather.

Parents are another excellent source of information, and they usually appreciate having the opportunity to tell you about their child. Surveys can be sent home or distributed at open house in the beginning of the school year. In the following space, begin developing questions for a parent survey:

Useful websites for student surveys include the following:

http://www.teachervision.fen.com/education-and-parents/printable/2282
    .html
http://www.orange.k12.nj.us/InclManualOrange/InclusionForms/STUDENT
    INTERESTINVENTORY-OrangeInclusionManual.pdf
http://www.saskschools.ca/curr_content/adapthandbook/learner/interest.html
http://teacher.scholastic.com/LessonPlans/unit_roadtosuccess_invent.pdf

Table 4.1. Survey information

Question to Ask	How Information Could Be Used

http://faculty.citadel.edu/hewett/web_files/interestweb.html
http://www.proteacher.net/discussions/showthread.php?t=10994

Additional survey sources on school and classroom climate include the following:

http://goal.learningpt.org/winss/scs/sampques.asp?survey=E
http://www.k12.wa.us/SchoolImprovement/pubdocs/PerceptionSurveys/
    IntSurv.doc
http://www.pike.k12.in.us/district/parents/ncaelementarysurvey.htm?g=29

DEVELOPING COOPERATION

Cooperation does not just happen. It takes time, planning, and practice. It is also an abstract idea and will be better understood by students if they have a chance to reflect on an actual cooperative experience. For example, use an easy puzzle of 12 pieces for a cooperation-building exercise. You can make this puzzle or perhaps find one in a store. You will need as many puzzles as you have groups of four in your classroom. If there are 24 students, you need six puzzles. Each student in the four-member group receives three puzzle pieces. At a signaled time, the group must work to put the puzzle together. They may not talk during this time. They may not take a piece from another player. They can only give a needed piece to another player.

At the end of the exercise, ask the students to define the term "cooperation." Have them offer suggestions as to what is needed for cooperation to take place. They may suggest that it is important that every member of the group have a clear understanding of the goal and that they are integral in achieving the goal. Each member must be aware of the actions and responsibilities of all other members in the group.

Let students suggest issues that need to be addressed and rules that need to be established when working cooperatively. Rules for cooperative groups might include the following: (a) each student must be willing to help anyone who needs help, (b) each student must be responsible for his or her own learning and actions, and (c) a student can ask the teacher a question only if all members of that group have the same question. This rule helps the group develop as a team to find an answer rather than immediately asking the teacher.

Cooperative groups work best if each member of the group has a job that holds them accountable in taking an active role. Jobs may include a monitor who keeps everyone on task, a writer who keeps notes on the discussion, a materials manager who is responsible to get any materials needed, a reporter who presents information orally, a thinking monitor who ensures that everyone has an opportunity to share, or any other position that the group activity requires. Let the students develop job titles and job descriptions. These can be written on index cards and distributed at the beginning of each cooperative group activity. This can also be used as a means to keep track of who had a specific job.

Keep in mind that group structure and membership change to accommodate the goal. This flexible grouping allows temporary groups to form that can change, expand, and develop to meet the needs of the assignment or activity. They can be developed based on skill, interests, needs, or student interactions. This method offers more differentiation to address student needs.

Websites for cooperative group activities include the following:

http://wilderdom.com/games/InitiativeGames.html
http://edtech.kennesaw.edu/intech/cooperativelearning.htm#activities
http://wilderdom.com/games/Icebreakers.html
http://www.education-world.com/a_curr/curr287a.shtml
http://www.utc.edu/Administration/WalkerTeachingResourceCenter/Faculty
    Development/CooperativeLearning/index.html

CLASS MEETINGS

Class meetings provide another method for developing cooperation and responsibility in a positive classroom environment. Depending on the grade level you work with, these meetings can take place daily or weekly. Structured around the issues or concerns of students, topics are discussed in an orderly problem-solving manner.

First, the problem must be identified. Students bring up the problem or issue to discuss by means of a suggestion box. Different age groups require strategies geared for that age group, but a good rule of thumb is that each suggestion or entry must be signed by the person posting the issue. This signature helps eliminate some inappropriate or ridiculous ideas. You might also want to suggest that people's names cannot be included in the problem.

After the issue is selected and read, the second step is to brainstorm possible solutions for the problem. To exchange ideas, students sit in a circular format and practice active listening and cooperative sharing. You may want to set a timer or clock to eliminate lengthy discussions. The third step includes a discussion of these ideas and a brainstorming of solutions. Fourth, students choose a solution, and finally they make a plan to implement the solution.

Through this practice, students are given ownership of their classroom community. They are empowered to address each problem, then develop and implement solutions.

Class meetings websites include the following:

http://www.sd83.bc.ca/classmtg/faq.html
http://www.proteacher.org/a/40174_Class_Meetings.html
http://www.nea.org/classmanagement/ifc020919.html
http://www.teachervision.fen.com/classroom-management/interpersonal-skills/
    4864.html
http://www.proteacher.com/cgi-bin/outsidesite.cgi?id=7354&external=
    http://www.sd83.bc.ca/classmtg/samples.html&original=http://www
    .proteacher.com/030006.shtml&title=Class%20Meeting%20Samples

SUMMARY

- You have the responsibility to develop a classroom climate that is conducive to learning.
- A classroom climate conducive to learning is one where everyone feels accepted and part of a community.

- Cooperation must be modeled and explicitly taught.
- Cooperation can be developed through the following:

Cooperative learning groups
Class meetings

ON YOUR OWN

Have you ever been in a situation in which you felt you did not belong? What was the situation? Why did you feel that you did not belong? How did you react to this feeling? What could have been done to alleviate the feeling?

FURTHER READING

Elementary Focus

Charney, R. S. (2002). *Teaching children to care: Classroom management for ethical and academic growth, K–8.* Greenfield, MA: Northeast Foundation for Children.

Emmer, E. T., & Gerwels, M. C. (2002). Cooperative learning in elementary classrooms: Teaching practices and lesson characteristics. *Elementary School Journal, 103*(1), 75–91.

Evertson, C. M., & Harris, A. H. (2003). *Creating conditions for learning: A comprehensive program for creating an effective learning environment* (6th ed.) Nashville: Peabody College, Vanderbilt University.

Freiberg, H. J. (1996). From tourists to citizens in the classroom. *Educational Leadership, 54,* 32–36.

Kim, D., Solomon, D., & Roberts, W. (1995, April). *Classroom practices that enhance students' sense of community.* Paper presented at the annual convention of the American Educational Research Association, San Francisco, CA.

Kohn, A. (1996). *Beyond discipline: From compliance to community.* Alexandria, VA: Association for Supervision and Curriculum Development.

Kriete, R. (2002). *The morning meeting book.* Greenfield, MA: Northeast Foundation for Children.

Martin, S. H. (2002). The classroom environment and its effects on the practice of teachers. *Journal of Environmental Psychology, 22,* 139–156.

Secondary Focus

Certo, J. L., Cauley, K., & Chafin, C. (2003, Winter). Students' perspectives on their high school experience. *Adolescence, 38,* 705–724.

Gay, G. (2006). Connections between classroom management and culturally responsive teaching. In C. M. Evertson & C. S. Weinstein (Eds.), *Handbook of classroom management: Research, practice, and contemporary issues* (pp. 343–370). Mahwah, NJ: Lawrence Erlbaum Associates.

Rodriguez, I. F. (2005). You, mister! *Educational Leadership, 62*(7), 78–80.

Rubin, B. C. (2003). Unpacking detracking: When progressive pedagogy meets students' social worlds. *American Educational Research Journal, 40*(2), 539–573.

Schaps, E. (2003). Creating a school community. *Educational Leadership, 60*(6), 31–33.

Spaulding, A. (2005). The impact of high school teacher behaviors on student aggression [computer file]. *Current Issues in Education, 8*(17), 1.

Tilleczek, K. (2007–2008). Building bridges: Transitions from elementary to secondary school. *Education Canada, 48*(1), 68–71.

Chapter Five

Fun

SITUATION

Juan continues to draw cartoons throughout the entire school day. I don't care what the subject is, he is drawing. At first, I took the drawings away from him. I also made him sit out during art so he could finish his work. I held a discussion with both him and his parents, and we agreed that this behavior could not continue. But nothing has changed. They didn't do anything at home to help me. How can I keep this student from drawing during class? Why aren't his parents more supportive of my efforts?

Situation Analysis

What would you recommend to this teacher? What steps could the teacher use to keep the student on task? How could this teacher elicit parent support? (Figure 5.1).

What comes to mind when you think of fun? Classroom fun could be humor and jokes, or it could be students enjoying being engaged in a relevant and useful learning experience. In the previous situation, is Juan enjoying the lesson? Is he engaged? How could the teacher use Juan's love for art to help him stay engaged in the lesson?

Jill: Our teacher talks to herself. Does yours?
Will: Yea, but he doesn't realize it. He thinks we are listening.

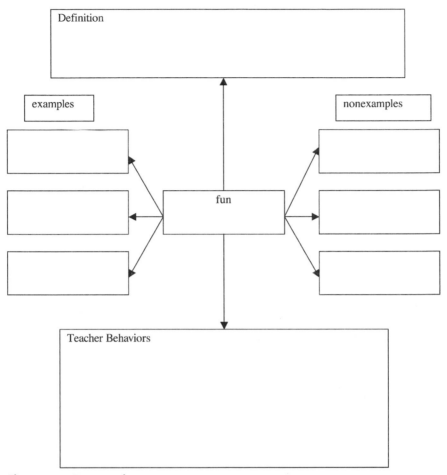

Figure 5.1.   Fun organizer

HUMOR

What do you consider humorous? Did you know that using humor can reduce test anxiety? It can build camaraderie, increase motivation, diffuse a stressful situation, and enhance creativity.

It is not necessary that you become a stand-up comedian. You just need to put a little enjoyment in the lesson. Try beginning the class with a humorous anecdote:

Knock knock
Who's there?

Acid.
Acid who?
Acid sit down and get to work!

Develop a funny picture board, humorous poetry, or enjoyable assignments. If you don't integrate humor and fun into the day, the students might create their own, and it probably will not be what you want in your class.

Claudia Cornett, in her *Learning Through Laughter—Again* (2001), provides the acronym SMILES for reasons to use humor in the classroom. Humor can ease *stress*, increase *motivation*, improve *image*, facilitate *learning*, provide salve to an *embarrassing* situation, and promote *social* bonding. She also suggests that by providing humor you are promoting higher-order thinking since humor involves a three-step process that includes "cognitive arousal, problem solving, and resolution" (p. 7).

There are many stressful situations in the classroom that could be eliminated if a little humor was injected or even if the situation was taken less seriously. Reprimands are not always needed, nor are they always the best approach.

Take, for example, that Steve comes into the classroom with a bad attitude. You know this because you are by the door greeting students as they enter. He grumps a greeting to you as he enters. A few minutes later, he slams a book on top of his desk and kicks another book across the room. Rather than a reprimand that provides him with another opportunity to strike out, you might just casually and quietly ask him if he needs some help defending himself against a book attack.

Why wasn't the clock allowed in the classroom?
Because it tocked too much.

Testing, behaviors, and the daily grind can cause stressful situations for students and teachers. Humor can help. Having fun doesn't mean out of control.

Read the following situations. How could you respond to diffuse the situation rather than enhance a confrontation?

Pat does not like to be told what to do. His defiant attitude has gotten him in trouble in the past. When you ask him to pick up the trash around his desk, he rudely and loudly responds, "I didn't put it there so I'm not picking it up."

Jake can be a very argumentative student. You have just given a lesson on Stonewall Jackson. In hopes of engaging the students more, you included the information that Jackson's arm is buried in a different place than his body. Jake loudly yells out, "I am not believing that. You are making that $@*& up."

You and Linda seem to be in a constant power struggle. After asking her group to line up for lunch, she saunters slowly in the back of the room and acts like she is arranging books on the bookshelf. She tries to sneak glances to see what you are going to do.

Nicholas has a tendency to be the class funny guy. Lately he has started making humorous comments after every assignment or direction you give to the class. It is becoming annoying and disruptive. After you assign several math problems to the class, you hear him in the back sarcastically stating, "Oh yeah, that is going to be real fun to do."

Humor websites include the following:

http://www.abbottcom.com/Humor_in_the_classroom.htm
http://www.faculty.armstrong.edu/roundtable/4717458.pdf
http://www.classroom-management.org/Using_Humor_To_Improve_Your_
    Classroom_Management.html
http://www.thecanadianteacher.com/tools/games
http://youth-activities.suite101.com/article.cfm/group_and_classroom_games
http://www.objectiveanalyst.com

Need some teacher humor?

http://teacherszine.tripod.com/teacherszine/id13.html
http://www.reacheverychild.com/feature/humor.html
http://www.teachersfirst.com/humor.shtml
http://www.edzone.net/~mwestern/funppt.html

ENGAGING STUDENTS

I once did a lesson on homophones in a language arts class. I was prepared to begin this lesson with an introduction to homophones using a picture book. I was feeling very good about this particular lesson since I was sure the students would be highly motivated and engaged. I used the picture book *The King Who Rained* by Fred Gwynne as an introduction. This is a fun book that provides illustrations of homophones so that students can visually interpret the double meaning.

On the front cover of the book, a king is high in the clouds with rain coming from his body, thus illustrating his rain (reign). As I held up the book to introduce the concept and began my wonderfully planned lesson, a student yelled from the back, "Oh my gosh, his water broke."

I had two choices. I could reprimand the student while reminding him of how inappropriate his comment was, or I could laugh along with the students. Fortunately, my inner teacher was in sync, and I was able to laugh and use this humor to move into the lesson. Without even knowing it, the student provided me with an excellent anticipatory set that got everyone engaged even if they didn't know what he was referring to with his comment about the water breaking. This humorous incident allowed me to capture the students' attention; however, I needed to keep that attention if learning was going to take place.

Jacob Kounin (1970) was one of the first psychologists to study the impact of effective lesson design and instruction on classroom management. He proposes that there is a clear relationship between the presentation of a lesson and student behavior. His studies indicate that you are better able to deliver instruction and maintain order through employing skills in momentum, with-it-ness, and ripple effect.

Momentum deals with the pacing of instruction in that the lesson begins promptly, moves students through the activity, and closes in a manner that brings about a smooth transition. Instruction is given at a pace that is neither too fast nor too slow. It is presented in an appropriate length of time so that it does not go on beyond the student's satiation level.

When you know what is going on in the classroom at all times, you can be termed as "with it." "With-it-ness" is a term coined by Kounin that suggests that you have "eyes in the back of the head." You are able to multitask and stay abreast of classroom happenings. You are able to stop the misbehavior before it spreads and escalates.

Kounin also introduced the term "ripple effect." This term refers to the effect that your comment or action to the individual can have on the entire group. To correct Eddie for not having his book out would motivate others to get their book out before you notice. It can also work in a positive manner. You compliment Bill for standing nicely in line, and soon all the other kindergartners quickly stand tall and face the front. The ripple effect works well with younger grades but has not been found successful with older students.

Although Kounin's ideas have been in use since the 1970s, his recommendations for classroom management are applicable to today's classrooms. Robert Marzano (2003) reported in his meta-analysis titled *The Critical Role of Classroom Management* that Kounin's studies and findings have been supported by subsequent studies. His acknowledgment of maintaining student interest and engagement to increase learning validates the need to have a repertoire of student engagement strategies.

Thumbs up or thumbs down is one easy technique to engage students during a whole-class discussion. After answering a question or making a statement, students must put their thumb up or down to indicate if they agree or

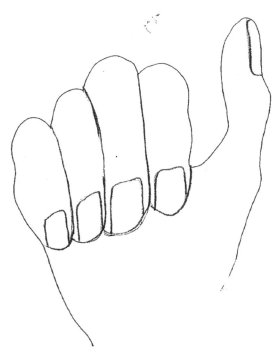

Figure 5.2.   Response thumb

not with what was said. Even if a student is not paying attention, this strategy
helps pull them back into the lesson. This technique also provides you with
immediate feedback on the level of student understanding. You can quickly
survey the room to determine who understands and who does not understand.
To prevent copying or following the crowd, you can supply each student with
a copy of a thumb that they can hold up or down to indicate their response
during classroom recitation (Figure 5.2).

What are some additional techniques you can use to keep students engaged
during a lesson?

Physical activities help in keeping students engaged; however, William
Glasser (1993) believes that quality teaching is essential for keeping students on task. He suggests, as discussed in chapter 3, that the classroom
environment be supportive and safe with clearly communicated objectives
and guidelines. In addition, learners need to be engaged in activities that are
purposeful and that will lead to knowledge that they deem useful and needed
to achieve a goal.

Quality teaching allows for students to work toward mastery yet lets them self-evaluate and redo. Glasser suggests the use of "SIR," or self-evaluate, improve, and repeat. Achievement promotes feelings and actions. Failure promotes destructive attitudes and behaviors.

Student engagement and motivation websites include the following:

http://www.nwrel.org/request/oct00/textonly.html
http://www.afcec.org/tipsforteachers/tips_b4.html
http://www.usp.edu/teaching/tips/spal.shtml
http://glossary.plasmalink.com/glossary.html
http://olc.spsd.sk.ca/DE/PD/instr/index.html

SUMMARY

- Classroom management and fun can coexist in the same classroom.
- Humor can diffuse stressful situations, keep students motivated, and enhance learning.
- Thirty years ago, management theorist Jacob Kounin introduced the ideas of the ripple effect and with-it-ness. These strategies are still relevant and effective practices.
- When students are engaged in the learning, they cause fewer behavior problems.
- Glasser suggests engaging students with quality teaching, which leads to student achievement. Student achievement leads to increased motivation.

ON YOUR OWN

Think back to one of your favorite teachers you had in school. Why is that teacher memorable? How successful were you in this teacher's class?

Can you think of an assignment or an activity from elementary or secondary school? Were you successful? Why? Why was the assignment important to you?

FURTHER READING

Elementary Focus

Christle, C. A., & Schuster, J. W. (2003). The effects of using response cards on student participation, academic achievement, and on-task behavior during whole-class, math instruction. *Journal of Applied Behavior Analysis, 12*(3), 147–165.

Nelson, K. (1999) A lesson they'll never forget! *Mailbox Teacher, 27*(4), 10–13.

Provine, R. (2000). *Laughter: A scientific investigation.* New York: Penguin.

Wanzer, M. B., & Frymier, A. B. (1999). The relationship between student perceptions for instructor humor and students' reports of learning. *Communication Education, 48,* 48–62.

Weaver, R. L., & Cotrell, H. W. (1986). Ten specific techniques for developing humor in the classroom. *Education, 108*(2), 167–179.

Secondary Focus

Brewster, C., & Fager, J. (2000). *Increasing student engagement and motivation: From time-on-task to homework.* Portland, OR: Northwest Regional Educational Laboratory. Available: http://www.nwrel.org/request/oct00/textonly.html

Intrator, S. M. (2004). The engaged classroom. *Educational Leadership, 62*(1), 20–24.

Minchew, S. S., & Hopper, P. (2008). Techniques for using humor and fun in the language arts classroom. *The Clearing House, 81*(5), 232–236.

Rea, D. W., Millican, K., & Watson, S. (2000). The serious benefits of fun in the classroom. *Middle School Journal, 31*(4), 23–28.

Shernoff, D. J., Czikszentmihalyi, M., Schneider, B., & Shernoff, E. S. (2003). Student engagement in high school classrooms from the perspective of flow theory. *School Psychology Quarterly, 18*(2), 158–176.

Starnes, B. A. (2007). The joke's on us. *Phi Delta Kappan, 88*(10), 793–794.

Walsh, J. A., & Sattes, B. D. (2005). *Quality questioning: Research-based practice to engage every learner.* Thousand Oaks, CA: Corwin Press.

Chapter Six

Freedom

SITUATION

Eli is a sixth-grade student who often comes in tardy and rarely has his materials or homework. He sits in the back of the room with his head on his desk, and he chooses not to engage in class discussions or interact with any students. He tends to blame other students and me for not doing his work. He actually told me that I was a terrible teacher and that it was my fault that he didn't have his homework. At least once a week, he tries to get out of doing his work by going to the school nurse. Either he has a rash or he develops a headache or some other excuse. Mrs. Barnhart, the nurse, told me yesterday the Eli may not come back to the clinic unless it is an emergency.

Situation Analysis

What is the problem in this scenario? What behavior in this situation needs to be addressed? (Figure 6.1).

When you consider freedom in the classroom, it probably brings images of something entirely different from what your students might suggest. For this text, freedom proposes that students are free to make choices in their academics and their behavior. In a well-managed classroom, freedom implies that students freely accept responsibility for their actions and hold themselves accountable for their learning.

Freedom might take the form of a student deciding which three academic assignments to complete out of the five suggested. It could suggest that students have the behavioral freedom to choose to complete their work during class or complete the unfinished work during the after-lunch "free time." One

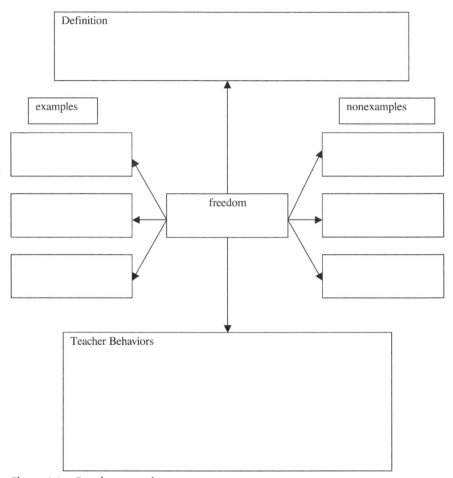

Figure 6.1. Freedom organizer

way to give students freedom is to empower them to make choices regarding their actions and their learning.

Freedom does not mean that you lack control; rather, by giving students some freedom, you are paradoxically both empowering and freeing yourself. By providing controlled freedom, you give the students a sense of ownership in their classroom and provide a structured environment for freedom to take place. Marzano (2003) suggests that this controlled yet free environment requires you to strike a balance between domination and cooperation.

Your domination of the classroom environment provides structure for learning to take place. You organize the lessons and plan the instruction. Practicing cooperation allows you to negotiate and work together with students in order to develop a community with shared ownership, responsibility, and commitment. Students then become free to make choices, accept responsibility, and remain accountable.

MAKING CHOICES

As discussed in part II of this text, William Glasser's choice theory suggests that student behavior is in response to a need or want and that a student chooses behavior based on the drive to satisfy the basic needs (survival, belonging, power, fun, and freedom). His ideas indicate that one person does not have control over another's behavior; rather, one can control only oneself.

If you accept Glasser's theory, then you accept the idea that you cannot control your students. You can, however, give them the information and opportunity to control and monitor their own behavior. He recommends that you never ask a student "why" they are choosing a certain behavior. "Why are you talking?" "Why are you out of your seat?" "Why" leads to excuses. Rather than ask why, you need to focus on what the student is doing. Ask the question, "What are you doing?" Once the behavior has been identified, the student can then evaluate the usefulness of the behavior. If the behavior is not useful in helping reach his goals, he is then able to develop a plan to change the behavior.

Glasser further explains teacher behaviors that help support students in making good decisions. He classifies these behaviors as the seven caring and the seven deadly habits. The seven caring habits include supporting, encouraging, listening, accepting, trusting, respecting, and negotiating differences. Through practicing these behaviors, you are better able to build a cooperation that leads to responsibility in good decision making.

The seven deadly habits are criticizing, blaming, complaining, nagging, threatening, punishing, and bribing or rewarding to control. When practiced, these behaviors negate a collaborative environment. They can lead to unmotivated and hostile students.

Glasser's websites include the following:

http://en.wikibooks.org/wiki/Classroom_Management_Theorist_and_
    Theories/William_Glasser
http://www.wglasser.com
http://raider.muc.edu/~schnelpl/Control%20Theory%20-%20Overhead.html
http://www.associatedcontent.com/article/404351/an_overview_of_dr_
    william_glassers.html

ACCEPTING RESPONSIBILITY

If your students do not make good choices in their behavior and actions, they need to understand the consequences that follow. Richard L. Curwin and Allen N. Mendler (1988) believe that students need to be taught they are responsible for their own behavior through the use of consequences rather than punishments. Consequences come about as a logical result of an action or lack of action. They can be either positive or negative, but either implies that a choice has been made. Punishment has a demeaning connotation. It is punitive and negative. Punishment takes away dignity and self-esteem.

Curwin and Mendler further support the idea that by giving students ownership in the classroom decisions, you promote discipline through dignity. By offering discipline through dignity, you demonstrate care about the student and show an understanding that the student's dignity and self-esteem must be motivated and maintained. Their ideas establish rules and consequences that create order in the classroom through a three-dimensional plan of prevention, action, and resolution.

Prevention or preventive discipline begins by building a management program that addresses your needs and the needs of your students. A well-established preventive program includes established rules that you and the students have developed together. These rules have been taught, practiced, and reinforced. The effective preventive program addresses not only the needs but also the diversities of your students. Prevention also includes the routines that establish predictability and consistency to the environment.

Action or supportive discipline refers to techniques you use to prevent escalating misbehavior or strategies you employ to support the student in making good choices. In the article "Twelve Practical Strategies to Prevent Behavioral Escalation in Classroom Settings," Shukla-Mehta & Albin (2003) provide 12 strategies to help prevent escalation in behavioral problems. They recommend that you know what triggers misbehavior.

Any day before a holiday will be a trigger. The day after Halloween will be a trigger. Spring, snow, and the full moon can all be added to the list. Any shift in the schedule can have a tendency to be a signal for misbehavior. If there is a change in behavior, it is important that you intervene early. Look for unusual behaviors or consistent patterns from a student.

The usual behaviors or consistent patterns help you identify the purpose behind the acting out. If consequences are warranted, use them wisely and judiciously. After you have taught and reinforced the appropriate behaviors for the classroom, provide opportunities for the students to be responsible and successful in their behaviors. Aim for being proactive rather than reactive. If the students are wound up, don't get wound up with them. Most importantly, choose your battles wisely. Not all misbehavior needs to be acknowledged or addressed.

The resolution or correction phase is needed when your preventive and supportive measures have not been successful. Corrective measures refer to the consequences you invoke to stop the misbehavior and get the student back on track while maintaining the student's dignity and your own well-being.

You might work on the "1-2-3 strikes you're out" technique. The student is given three chances with some type of indicator as to how many strikes or chances the student currently has already used. This could be in the form of name on the board, stoplight fixture, color-coded card, or a baseball diamond. There are numerous adaptations to this idea, and which one you use does not really matter except that it needs to be something the students will accept and follow.

Canter (1992) recommends using five consequential steps in his assertive discipline program. In this positive approach, teachers establish clear guidelines that allow for teaching and learning to take place. By establishing rules, setting limits, and following through with consequences, you are able to maintain a positive, caring, and productive environment.

Canter (1989) suggests that a positive attitude is the key to dealing effectively with misbehavior. He recommends using assertiveness along with positive reinforcements and praise to teach students how to behave. Each student should be complimented at least one time during the school day.

If you develop a consequence model, you will want to insert a means of redemption. If a student gets three or five strikes in the first half hour of school, there is nothing to encourage him to behave the rest of the day unless there is some way to redeem himself.

What about consequences or interventions? In an effective classroom management plan, consequences might be necessary to intervene and, it is hoped, bring about the desired behavior. For example, as an intervention strategy, you might remove the disruptive child from the class. This might seem like an appropriate solution since you get a break from the student and the student stops the behavior, but actually the student is being removed from the learning environment. Since the whole point of having a well-managed, disciplined classroom is to increase learning, this does not seem to be a logical action. Perhaps a brief time-out in the classroom might be more appropriate.

Use the following space to brainstorm appropriate consequences for when a rule is broken:

First offense:

Second offense:

Third offense:

Fourth offense:

Fifth offense:

Would you have three strikes per week or three strikes per day? How would the age level of the student impact the length of time allotted for three strikes?

Try several interventions or consequences prior to calling home and work with the parents or caregivers prior to sending a child to the office. If you have to send a child to the office, make sure that you have exhausted your classroom program, conferred previously with the caregiver of the student, and documented all efforts. Administrators cannot do their job if you have not done yours.

ACCOUNTABILITY

Accountability occurs when students know that their work will be checked and evaluated. It is brought about by clear instructions, adequate monitoring, and valuable feedback. Students need to know exactly what is expected of them in each assignment. They need to know the format, dates, expectations, and grading procedures.

I gave a 6-week book report assignment once to a group of fourth graders. Here are the directions that I gave the students:

Select one biography from the library.
Read the book carefully to determine the major events in this person's life.
Develop a three-dimensional scene depicting an event in this person's life.
Write a three-page report that summarizes the book.

I was addressing many standards with this assignment and felt like I could cover a great deal of content through this biography assignment. At the end of the 6 weeks, I received not one book report. This was not a case of student failure; the one common denominator here was me, so I had to take a look at my instructions. First of all, there had been no instruction. I merely gave directions that were unclear and misunderstood.

What I should have done was to introduce the concept of biographical literature. I would start by making it personal to them and have them develop a time line of the major events in their lives. This would be followed by a summary of the three major events.

I would probably read a biography out loud to the class and have them identify the major events in the person's life as we read along. After the biography was finished, I would model identifying major events, demonstrate depicting a scene, and teach summarizing and writing skills. The school librarian would be asked to pull biographies on reading level and interest to fourth graders. After the book had been approved by me, I would allow in-class reading time and monitor their progress through assignments, discussions, and updates. The assignment would cover a 2-week time period and would include the scene, a time line, and a report. The report would be one page that describes the event that was created and why the student selected that particular event to depict.

Read the following instructions given to a fourth-grade class regarding a social studies project:

> You will need to build a model that depicts an event that occurred in Philadelphia during the American Revolution. Along with the model, you will need to write a one-page paper explaining WHO, WHAT, WHEN, and WHERE about your event. This project is due on May 4.

What questions come to mind as you read these instructions?

What else needs to be included in the directions?

What steps would you take to monitor the student progress?

How would the project be graded? What are the criteria?

Rewrite the instructions to establish clear guidelines of expectations for the assignment.

Students must realize that they will be held accountable for their behavior. As with academic work, the expectations need to be made clear and consequences consistent. Self-evaluations provide an excellent venue for giving students the ownership of their behavior. One of the consequences for misbehavior could be the completion of a self-evaluation form. By filling out a self-evaluation, you have a document of the behavior and a plan for improvement. The following websites provide examples of self-evaluation forms you can use in the classroom:

http://www.teachervision.fen.com/classroom-discipline/resource/6283.html
http://www.busyteacherscafe.com/wspages/forms.htm
http://freeology.com/formsforteachers
http://www.gigglepotz.com/forms.htm

SUMMARY

- Students need to feel they have the freedom to make choices both academically and behaviorally.
- Your role is to strike a balance between domination and cooperation.
- Support students in making good choices through practicing the seven caring habits.
- Practice three methods of discipline: preventive, supportive, and corrective:

  Help prevent misbehavior through successful classroom management
  Help support appropriate behavior by offering initiatives
  Help correct the misbehavior when it occurs

- With the opportunity to make choices comes the need to accept responsibility for those choices.
- Students need to be held accountable for their academics and behavior through efficient management and instruction skills.

ON YOUR OWN

Behavior and instruction are so closely linked that it is sometimes difficult to separate them. Can you think of any situations where behavior and instruction should not be interdependent? Should a student receive the same consequence for not bringing in his homework as he does for causing a classroom disruption? Why or why not?

FURTHER READING

Elementary Focus

Canter, L., & Canter, M. (2001). *Assertive discipline: Positive behavior management for today's classroom* (3rd ed.). Santa Monica, CA: Lee Canter & Associates.

Kohn, A. (March). Almost there, but not quite. *Educational Leadership, 60*(6), 26–29.

Marshall, M. L. (March). Fostering social responsibility and handling disruptive classroom behavior. *NASSP Bulletin, 82,* 31–39.

Power, C. (2006). Developing self-discipline and preventing and correcting misbehavior. *Journal of Moral Education, 35*(3), 420–423.

van Lier, P. A. C., Muthen, B. O., Vander Sar, R. M., & Crijnen, A. A. M. (2004). Preventing disruptive behavior in elementary schoolchildren: Impact of a universal classroom-based intervention. *Journal of Consulting and Clinical Psychology* Jun; 72(3): 467–78.

Secondary Focus

Creating caring schools. (2003). *Educational Leadership, 60*(6).

DePry, R. L., & Sugai, G. (2002). The effects of active supervision and precorrection on minor behavioral incidents in a sixth grade general education classroom. *Journal of Behavioral Education, 11,* 255–264.

Little, S. G., & Alkin-Little, A. (2008). Psychology's contributions to classroom management. *Psychology in the Schools, 45*(3), 227–234.

Marshall, M. (2005). Discipline without stress, punishments, or rewards. *The Clearing House, 79*(1), 51–54.

Martin, N. K. (1997). Connecting instruction and management in a student-centered classroom. *Middle School Journal, 28,* 3–9.

Zuckerman, J. T. (2007). Classroom management in secondary schools: A study of student teachers' successful strategies. *American Secondary Education, 35*(2), 4–16.

Chapter Seven

Power

SITUATION

Today is Sophie's seventh birthday. This morning before she left for school, her parents gave her a new sticker book. Unfortunately, they did not make sure she kept the book at home, and here she is in math class playing with the stickers. I have already told her twice to put them away, so this time I quickly walk to her desk and take the book. She immediately bursts into tears. Now the rest of the class is looking at us, and nobody is doing their work.

Situation Analysis

What are you going to do? What could have helped prevent the situation? What, if anything, should you do about the book? The tears?

In the situation of Sophie, the teacher has the power to take away the book. But what has been achieved? The purpose of taking the book is supposedly to get Sophie working on her math. Unfortunately, in the process of taking the stickers, the teacher has taken Sophie's mind further from the math lesson. Not only was Sophie off task, but now the entire class is not thinking of math. In reality, who has the most power in this situation? (Figure 7.1).

Control and strength come to mind when I think of power. Power assumes authority or the ability to cause an effect. Student power is demonstrated not as the ability to control other people but, rather, as the ability to control self. Teacher power is demonstrated not as authority to dominate the student's will but, rather, as motivating students to make good choices. Communication and success provide the foundations of power. This chapter explores the acquisition of teacher power through effective communication skills and student power through achievement.

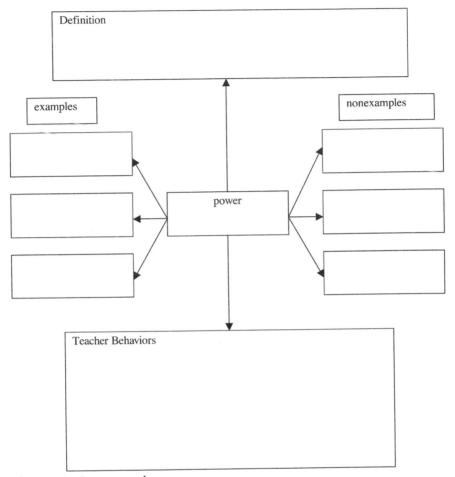

Figure 7.1.   Power organizer

TEACHER POWER THROUGH COMMUNICATION

Communicating with Students

The amount of power you gain in the classroom is as a direct result of how you are viewed by your students, and their perceptions are developed around the effectiveness of your communication. Your communication style has the ability to build or destroy. It is important that you come to terms with your own power and not engage in classroom power struggles.

When you verbally engage in a power struggle or argue with a student, you lose. Regardless of who has detention or has time-out, you have lost. Your best approach is to detach from the situation and remain calm. You might need a mental "time-out" before you address the problem.

Fredric Jones (1987) suggests that body language is an essential component of communication and effective classroom management. You can communicate support for your student's attempts at self-discipline through your use of body language in facial gestures, preestablished signals, and physical proximity. For example, if Jeffry is across the room misbehaving while you are with the reading group, perhaps a "look" or a raised finger would offer the support that he needs to get back on track. If this doesn't work, you might need to move closer to him or maybe put a hand on his shoulder. The less disruption that is caused for the entire class is the best route to take.

When you do need to discuss a behavior, address the specific behavior and not the student. Communicate the idea that the behavior, not the student, is inappropriate. Discuss the action privately rather than across the room or in front of a group.

Hiam Ginott (1972) provides communication strategies in his writings on congruent communication. He suggests that you can offer dignity to your students rather than assign blame or guilt. Rather than stating, "Emma, you are not listening to Annie's report!" you could use a sane message, such as, "Emma, you are expected to sit quietly and listen while Annie gives her report."

Rather than demanding certain behaviors from students, Ginott suggests that you will have more power by inviting cooperation, such as stating, "All students who complete the assigned homework will be able to use the last 20 minutes of class as game time" rather than saying, "All students who don't complete the assigned homework will have detention."

You have the ability to build rapport and gain power with your students through the communication that you use. "I" messages rather than "you" messages allow you to acknowledge your feelings about a situation rather than put blame on the student. Thomas Gordon (1974) identifies three parts in an "I" statement: problem identification, problem effect, and teacher feelings. Let's say that Bud is having a bad morning and comes in angrily and noisily. He sneers at Sammy and calls him a bad name. Rather than blaming Bud for hurting Sammy's feelings, you could state, "When a student comes in angrily and noisily, other students are hurt, and that upsets me." This will get a more positive reaction and help build relationships rather than barriers.

Read the following teacher statements and rewrite each to indicate an "I" message:

Pam, you do not have your homework again.

Brenda, you have been told 100 times that passing notes in class is not allowed.

You guys did not behave in the assembly.

Ron, quit talking and get to work.

The entire class was horrible for the substitute yesterday.

Communicating with Parents

Start off the school year by contacting the parents with a positive telephone call. Let the parent know how pleased you are to have their child in your classroom and how you look forward to a successful year. This one phone call will make a difference when you need to contact them later because of a negative issue or concern. Keep parents aware of what is going on academically in the classroom through the use of newsletters or a Web page.

When you are meeting with a parent, make sure you prepare a discussion "sandwich." Start with a positive comment, sandwich the issue or problem in the middle, and end with a positive comment and recommendation. Most parents or caregivers want to know what is going on with their child, but they do not want their time wasted by petty complaints or unprepared teachers. If you are speaking with a caregiver, be prepared with an agenda and examples. Allow the caregiver or parent to give input. Log every contact. Document what was said and any agreed-on intervention strategies to put into place.

If you are confronted with angry parents or caregivers, first make them feel comfortable and start with a positive. Allow them to vent their frustrations while maintaining an empathic attitude. Practice active listening while keeping eye contact. Try to reach an agreement and end on a positive note. If the conference becomes abusive, end it quickly and tactfully.

Read each of the following situations. How would you respond to each parent?

Mrs. Exum has recently taken her daughter Kasey off Ritalin. Although she agrees that Kasey is able to stay on task and is better focused with the medication, she does not want her daughter on the medication. She insists that Kasey will become addicted to the medication and that it will lead to other drugs. Kasey's grades have dropped dramatically since she has been off the medication. You are concerned that if something is not done soon, Kasey will fall behind and not be able to catch up. You have called a conference with the mother. As she enters the room, she loudly states, "If you had more interesting lessons, my daughter would be able to pay attention."

LaShonda Jones's mother calls you one evening around 10:00. She insists on meeting with you the next day but then realizes that she has to work. You agree to discuss the situation on the phone. She proceeds to explain to you that LaShonda's father died 2 years ago and that it is LaShonda's responsibility to take care of her three younger siblings when she gets home from school. Mrs. Jones wants you to relieve LaShonda from any homework so that she can take care of her duties at home. She begins to explain what caused the death of her husband. At 10:30 she is beginning to go into detail about the difficult birth of her fourth child, and LaShonda's problem has not been discussed. You are tired and want to get off the phone.

Mike Grose is one of those students who is constantly bothering the other students during lessons. He takes their pencils and breaks them, their paper and writes on it, or their belongings and hides them. He is either tapping his pencil on his desk, humming, or rocking back in his chair. Last week he fell over backward at his desk. He is disturbing the entire class and agitating the students who sit near him. You have contacted his parents for a conference. Mr. Grose shows up at your door one Friday afternoon as you are just about to leave. You politely explain the trouble that Mike has caused. The father gets a rather quizzical look on his face and asks, "So what do you want me to do? It is your problem."

Effective communication websites include the following:

http://www.khake.com/page66.html
http://www.teacherhelp.org/classroommgnt.htm#parents
http://www.uncg.edu/~bblevin/class_management/moremodels/HaimGinott.html

STUDENT POWER THROUGH SUCCESS

Give power to students by providing opportunities for their success. Power comes through the feeling of achievement. Allow students the opportunity to succeed by mastering their behavior and their learning. The more success the student experiences, the more engaged he or she will be in the learning. The more engaged the student is in the learning process, the less opportunity and desire he or she will have for misbehavior.

You have the most influence on your students' learning (Marzano, Pickering, & Pollock, 2001) and therefore have the power to structure instruction that ensures student success. In her book *Improving Student Learning One Teacher at a Time*, Jane Pollock (2007) outlines principles for students' learning success in "the big four." Her recommendations for developing master learners include the use of clearly stated learning targets, effective instructional strategies, variety of assessments, and specific feedback.

The clearly stated learning targets are stated in understandable terms that align with the state standards. They are written in a manner that connects the broad curriculum to useful understandings rather than specific behaviors. These targets or objectives are also written to correspond with either declarative or procedural knowledge. If you are targeting declarative or content knowledge, you would use words such as "understands" or "knows." If you are targeting procedural or skill-based knowledge, you would focus more on action verbs that indicate a behavior.

In his book *What Works in Schools*, Robert Marzano (2003b) outlines the results of a meta-analysis of researched effective instructional strategies. He suggests that the following nine categories of instructional strategies are the most affective in promoting student achievement:

- Identifying similarities and differences
- Summarizing and note taking
- Reinforcing effort and providing recognition
- Homework and practice
- Nonlinguistic representation
- Cooperative learning
- Setting objectives and providing feedback
- Generating and testing hypotheses
- Questions, cues, and advance organizers

Use the following sources to develop a brief description and a classroom example for each of the instructional strategies listed:

http://www.middleweb.com/MWLresources/marzchat1.html
http://manila.esu6.org/instructionalstrategies
http://162.127.6.150/Gems/instructionalstrat/NETAInstStrat.ppt

Identifying similarities and differences:

Summarizing and note taking:

Reinforcing effort and providing recognition:

Homework and practice:

Nonlinguistic representation:

Cooperative learning:

Setting objectives and providing feedback:

Generating and testing hypotheses:

Questions, cues, and advance organizers:

Additional websites for instructional strategies include the following:

http://www.cpt.fsu.edu/ese/in/strmain.html
http://glossary.plasmalink.com/glossary.html

http://ims.ode.state.oh.us/ode/ims/rrt/research/Topic_Using_Effective_
    Instructional_Strategies.asp
http://www.greece.k12.ny.us/instruction/ela/6-12/essentialskills.htm
http://www.k12.dc.us/DCPS/curriculum/instruction/tools/t-is.pdf
http://volcano.und.edu/vwdocs/msh/llc/is/is.html

As an integral part of the student learning, assessment can be used to diagnose the student's strengths and weaknesses, monitor student progress, assign
grades, and determine your instructional effectiveness. To diagnose and obtain information about a student's level of performance, Pollock (2007) suggests that classroom assessment techniques can be divided into the following
three areas: testing for recall, testing for thinking, and observation and self-
assessment. Each of these strategies provides valuable information to guide
instruction and should be employed to assess correlating benchmarks.

Describe a situation in which each of the following would be used:

Testing for recall:

Testing for thinking:

Observation and self-assessment:

Both informal and formal assessment tools can be used to obtain the needed
information in each of these techniques. In testing recall, you can informally
use class questioning and recitation to assess the student's knowledge, or you
could formally assess recall through the use of a teacher-made test. The focus
here is to offer a variety of assessment opportunities. The use of multiple
strategies provides the students with various means to show mastery.

If assessment is used to gauge student performance and guide instruction,
you must provide students with criterion-based feedback that will lead them
into additional practice and improvement. Criterion-based feedback offers
suggestions and comments that are directly related to the criterion you have
established in your benchmarks. Only through the immediate and specific
feedback can you guide your students into success. Rather than comments
such as "good job," provide feedback that addresses a specific component of

the assignment that was well done or the specific characteristic that made the assignment "well done."

Useful assessment websites include the following:

http://school.discoveryeducation.com/schrockguide/assess.html
http://www.eed.state.ak.us/tls/frameworks/mathsci/ms5_2as1.htm
http://www.rmcdenver.com/useguide/assessme/definiti.htm
http://www.rmcdenver.com/useguide/assessme/online.htm

SUMMARY

- You have the power to motivate students to make good choices.
- Your power is in direct proportion to your communication skills.
- Effective communication skills are needed with both parents and students and involve issues such as the following:

    Body language
    Inviting cooperation
    "I" messages

- Students gain power through success and achievement.
- Robert Marzano found the following instructional strategies to be most effective in helping students achieve:

    Identifying similarities and differences
    Summarizing and note taking
    Reinforcing effort and providing recognition
    Homework and practice
    Nonlinguistic representation
    Cooperative learning
    Setting objectives and providing feedback
    Generating and testing hypotheses
    Questions, cues, and advance organizers

ON YOUR OWN

What advantages do you see as a result of involving parents in your classroom? When would it be most advantageous to have parent involvement? What challenges do you see in involving parents in your classroom? When would you not want to involve a parent or parents?

FURTHER READING

Elementary Focus

Bailey, J. M., & Guskey, T. R. (2001). *Implementing student-led conferences.* Thousand Oaks, CA: Corwin Press.

Brookfield, S. D., & Preskill, S. (2005). *Discussion as a way of teaching: Tools and techniques for democratic classrooms* (2nd ed.). San Francisco: Jossey-Bass.

Drummond, K. V., & Stipek, D. (2004). Low-income parents' beliefs about their role in children's academic learning. *Elementary School Journal, 104*(3), 197–213.

Minke, K. M., & Anderson, K. J. (2003). Restructuring routine parent-teacher conferences: The family-school conference model. *Elementary School Journal, 104*(6), 49–69.

Nelson, J. L., Lott, L., & Glenn, H. S. (2000). *Positive discipline in the classroom* (3rd ed.). Roseville, CA: Prima.

Secondary Focus

Corbett, D., Wilson, B., & Williams, B. (2005). No choice but success. *Educational Leadership, 62*(6), 8–12.

Marzano, R. J., & Marzano, J. (2003). The key to classroom management. *Educational Leadership, 61*(1), 6–13.

Protheroe, N. (2004). Effective teaching. *Principal, 83*(4), 58–60, 62.

Umphrey, J. (2008). Producing learning: A conversation with Robert Marzano. *Principal Leadership* (High School Ed.), *8*(5), 16–20.

Vaughan, A. L. (2005). The self-paced student. *Educational Leadership, 62*(7), 69–73.

Chapter Eight

Meeting Special Needs*

You have learned methods that are effective in meeting the basic needs of students you encounter in your classrooms. But some students, the "tough kids," have needs that are much more complicated and intense than those of average students. These needs, which can relate to academic, behavioral or social deficits, are so strong that they keep the student from responding to the system of consequences that is present in most good classrooms. Because the students have a harder time performing the required tasks for various reasons, those consequences are not powerful enough to cause them to put forth the extreme effort necessary for success (Bateman & Golly, 2003). A different, more systematic program is necessary to help these students experience success in the classroom.

The need for a systematic program, or behavior plan, can apply to an entire classroom that has developed resistant negative behavior patterns, a few students who have similar behavioral challenges, or individual "tough kids." The following examples and exercises will help you understand how to apply the steps in this program, giving you a tool that will empower you to teach all your students, even the most difficult ones.

SITUATION 1

It is the beginning of a new school year, and already Rachel knows that her third-grade class will be challenging. Last year she put into place the new behavior management methods she learned, and they worked very well. She set

---

*This chapter was written by Dr. Norah Hooper, Associate Professor of Education and Special Education Program Coordinator at the University of Mary Washington.

rules, worked at meeting student needs, was consistent with consequences, and was rewarded with a smooth-running classroom. It was a pleasure to come to school each day, and she was confident that her students made good academic progress.

Her group this year is different. Even in the first week, Rachel sees that they are quite active and noisy. They almost never raise their hands, as they continually call out answers and questions during instruction periods. When they should be working independently, they speak to each other and to her across the room, asking for help or just carrying on conversations. They helped set the rule about raising hands and speaking quietly, and she reminds them often, but they continue to clamor loudly for her attention.

She finds herself moving from group to group in response to their requests, answering questions and continually asking them to quiet down. She tries reasoning with them, taking away recess, and promising a party on Friday if they are quiet, but nothing works. She is very frustrated with the high level of noise and low level of productivity in her class.

Rachel decides that she needs some help, so she consults her behavior specialist, Angela. Angela comes and observes her classroom for a morning, and Rachel is both relieved and embarrassed that her students demonstrate their characteristic noisy behavior. In their after-school discussion, Angela tells Rachel that her well-organized behavior program works well in most cases but that there are times when a specific student or the whole group has certain characteristics that require more intensive programs.

While there is not one specifically challenged student in her room who is causing trouble, the mix of students this year has resulted in a very noisy group. She surprises Rachel by telling her that her own actions may be reinforcing these noisy behaviors so that her attempts to get them to quiet down are making them more vocal.

Situation Analysis

What is the problem in Rachel's situation? Are the students' needs being met? What could be causing the group to be so different from last year's? What type of solution do you think Angela will propose?

Table 8.1. Steps in Developing a Behavior Plan

Step 1	Define the problem behavior
Step 2	Gather information about the behavior
Step 3	Determine what is maintaining the behavior
Step 4	Develop a plan
Step 5	Implement the plan
Step 6	Monitor the plan

Angela describes the steps involved in developing a behavior plan (Table 8.1). Essentially, she said, the process involves answering two questions: "Why do they do that?" and "How can I get them to stop?" Together, she and Rachel examine these steps in relation to her classroom problem.

Step 1: Define the Problem Behavior

How would you define the behavior that is causing problems in Angela's classroom? It is important to be very specific about the student actions that you want to change:

The problem behavior seems obvious at first, but when Angela tells Rachel that she will need to measure the students' actions, she realizes that she needs to be very exact. Surprisingly, it is often difficult to pinpoint the exact behavior that you are trying to change (Alberto & Troutman, 2006). Rachel decides that a "call out" will be counted any time students speak out loud without first being given permission by her. They can get permission by raising their hand and waiting to be acknowledged before speaking. If a student speaks out while raising a hand, it is still considered a "call out."

Step 2: Gather Information About the Behavior

What else do you think Rachel needs to know about what is happening in her classroom? How can she find out?

Angela's observation was a first step in gaining new information about what was happening in Rachel's classroom. She noticed that the students got louder when Rachel was speaking and that the number of call outs during independent work time was higher than during active class activities. She observed Rachel's behavior as well as that of the students, and she saw that whenever a student called out, Rachel gave attention to that student. Sometimes she answered his question or acknowledged that his answer was correct. Other times she scolded the student for calling out or reminded her about the possibility of losing recess. Whenever they vocalized out loud, they got a response from Rachel. Because she was so busy responding to those who called out, she had no time to pay attention to the quiet students.

Step 3: Determine What Is Maintaining the Behavior

Based on the information Angela gathered, what might be concluded about what is maintaining the noisy behavior of the students? Should she get more information? How can she get it?

Every behavior is performed for a reason, and the behavior is repeated because it meets a need. The reason for the behavior is also called the function, or the purpose it is serving for the student. These will often fall into two categories: the student needs to either get something or escape from something(Mallot, 2008). In this case, Angela tells Rachel, the students are calling out to get her attention. She said that it is likely that Rachel's responses, both positive and negative, were serving as *reinforcers* and maintaining or even increasing the calling-out behaviors.

The students experienced all responses from their teacher, even those she thought of as negative consequences, such as threatening to take away recess, as reinforcers. Her actions made them want to do it more, and they did. Part of the reason for this was that the Rachel's negative response was more predictable and consistent than was her praise (Oliver & Reschly, 2007). The quiet students quickly became noisy since they saw that only loud behavior got Rachel's attention.

Step 4: Develop a Plan

What type of plan would you develop? What are the parts to the plan? How would you be sure to stick with the plan?

Angela says that this type of situation is relatively common in classrooms and not too difficult to fix. Together they develop a plan. First, Rachel will count the number of call outs in a specific time period to give her a basis for comparison. She will then use two techniques: *extinction*, or the removal of a previously used reinforcement, and *differential reinforcement of a lower rate of behavior*. She will no longer respond to people who call out (extinction). Instead, she will answer only those who raise their hand (Table 8.2).

She will continue to count the number of call outs, and on every day that the number is below a certain level (to be set after she does her counting), the students will have an extra 10 minutes of free time at the end of the day. Angela cautions her to set this number at a level she thinks they can achieve

Table 8.2.   Changing Behavior

Definition	Examples
Increasing behavior	
Positive reinforcement—providing a consequence following a behavior that increases the rate or strength of that behavior.	"Read this book, and I will give you a prize." "Eat your vegetables, and you can have dessert." (These are considered reinforcements only if the person reads the book or eats the vegetables.)
Negative reinforcement—removing or reducing the strength of an environmental condition (usually something unpleasant), increasing a behavior's rate or strength. A person does what you ask in order to escape an uncomfortable situation.	Mike's mother nags him about making his bed, so he does it to get her to stop bugging him. Beth is worried about doing well on a test, so she studies until she feels prepared. (Mike and Beth are motivated by the need for escape [from the nagging and from the scared feeling], so they perform the task.)
Decreasing behavior	
Punishment—providing a consequence following a behavior that decreases the rate or strength of that behavior.	John is sent to his room because he teases his sister. Martha gets detention for several tardies. (These are only considered punishments only if John dislikes being sent to his room enough to stop teasing and if Martha starts getting to class on time.)
Differential reinforcement for lower rates of behavior or differential reinforcement for omission of behavior—providing a positive consequence for doing less of a behavior or not doing it at all.	Mary has the habit of sharpening her pencil several times each day. You reward her for doing it twice each day or less. Tony, who tends to get in fights, is rewarded each day that he does not fight.
Differential reinforcement for alternate behavior—providing a positive consequence for doing a different behavior that serves the same purpose as the offensive behavior.	You reward Sam for asking for help with math instead throwing his math book on the floor. You reward the class for lining up without a sound instead of chattering as they go to the door.
Extinction—removing the consequence that is maintaining the behavior.	Eric's mother stops laughing at his inappropriate jokes, and he stops telling them. The teacher ignores Mark's whining and instead responds quickly when he speaks appropriately—for a while, he whines even

(continued)

Table 8.2. (*continued*)

Definition	Examples
	more, but she persists and eventually he stops.
	(Ignoring, or taking away a reinforcement, is sometimes tricky, as it is important to understand what is maintaining the behavior, and it often gets worse before it gets better.)

relatively quickly so that they can experience the pleasure of the reward. Rachel decides to lower it as their behavior improves.

She knows that they value this free time since they have been willing to work for it in the past, and she believes that the time saved in dealing with the noise level will result in at least 10 more minutes of instructional time. She will also display the number of call outs on a large graph, making the students aware of their own behavior.

Step 5: Implement the Plan

What do you think of this plan? What other plan might Rachel use to change the noisy behavior of the students? How can Rachel teach and count behavior at the same time? List at least five ways:

Before describing the plan to the students, Rachel needs to count the *frequency* of the call outs (Table 8.3). She decides to do this for 3 days as a baseline during the first 90-minute period of the day, when students are doing reading and writing. Angela describes an easy counting method that doesn't require carrying a clipboard around the room. Rachel wears pants or a skirt with pockets, and she puts some dried beans in her right pocket. Whenever a student calls out, she shifts a bean to her left pocket. At the end of the period, she counts the beans in her left pocket and records the results on a chart (Table 8.4). The first day there are 35 beans, the second there are 42, and on the third there are 39.

After getting these baseline numbers, Rachel starts the plan. She talks to the students about the problem and tells them that things are going to change in the classroom. They will get no response for call outs, only for raised hands and quiet work. If they have fewer than 15 call outs in a morning, they get

Table 8.3. Measuring Behaviors

Behavior samples—data collected while the behavior is taking place

Frequency—count the number of times a behavior is performed (while it is being done)	Count the number of times Allen gets out of his seat Count the number of times Susan taps her pencil
Duration—measure how long a behavior lasts	See how long Judy spends in the bathroom Measure how long it takes Mike to complete a math paper
Intensity—measure the strength of behavior	Use a rating scale to determine the intensity of John's tantrum

Data collected after behavior has occurred

Permanent product—count or measure something in the absence of the student	Count number of worksheets completed Count number of items left on the floor
Locus—record where a behavior has occurred	Note the classes in which Mike had outbursts each day

Table 8.4. Data Collection Form

	Number of Call Outs
Baseline	35
	42
	39
Intervention	
First week	36
	33
	21
	20
	15
Second week	13
	13
	10
	10
Third week	8
	5
	4
	4
	2
	3
	2

extra free time in the afternoon. The students respond surprisingly well to the plan, and she realizes that they were no happier with the noisy room than she was. They just needed consistent, systematic help in making a change.

Rachel finds that it is tough at first to change her own behavior and ignore those who call out. She has to look carefully for the quiet ones and to respond quickly to a raised hand—just as quickly as she previously responded to a loud voice. She keeps counting, and the numbers start to go down: 36 beans in the left pocket the first day of the plan, 33 the second, and 21 the third. By Friday they have earned the reward, and everyone is happier with the quieter classroom.

Step 6: Monitor the Results

What should Rachel do now? Is the problem fixed? How do you think she can help the students maintain the new behavior?

With Angela's help, Rachel is careful to stick with the plan even though she achieved quick results. It will be easy for all of them to slip back into old patterns. She continues to count and ignore call outs (much easier now since the number is lower) and to provide the reward for a quiet morning. Interestingly, she finds that the quiet classroom itself is a reward to almost everyone, as they can work more efficiently and get their questions answered without having to make noise. As an extra incentive for both her and the students, Rachel posts the results of her tallies on a graph. The descending line reminds all of them that the plan is working (Figure 8.1).

By the end of the third week, she changes the criterion so that the students have to have fewer than five call outs to earn the reward. They are meeting it every day and are delighted with the graphic evidence of their improvement. They are accomplishing more work than ever, even with their 10 minutes of afternoon free time. Rachel is very pleased with the results of her collaboration with Angela and her ability to develop and implement a behavior intervention plan successfully. She learned how to manipulate consequences of behaviors in a systematic and consistent way that benefited everyone.

SITUATION 2

Mary is frustrated with the behavior of a small group of students in her class because they are not turning in homework. Although she is assigning work

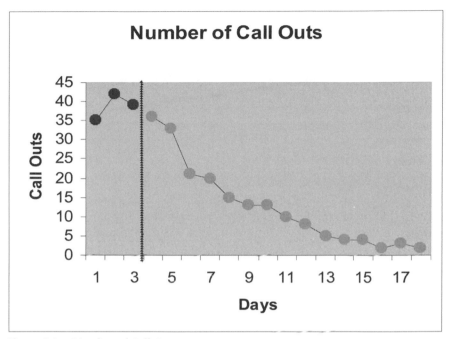

Figure 8.1. Number of Call Outs

that they are able to do independently, five or six students are coming in day after day without their homework. She has been blaming the parents for being disorganized and students for a lack of motivation, but after hearing more about behavior plans, she is wondering if there is something she can do in her classroom to increase the level of homework completion. She decides to go through the steps of the behavior plan, seeking Angela's help if necessary.

Rachel learned to decrease an unwanted behavior, but Mary is trying to do the opposite—increase the number of times a student does something. What are some ways that work to get people to increase the number of times they do something?

Step 1: Define the Problem Behavior

How would you define this behavior? How would you measure it? Name three different ways to measure homework completion:

If a student hands in completed homework assignments, Mary records them in her grade book with a checkmark. She does not grade homework. She needs to be clear about incomplete assignments, though, and decides that they must be complete: an assignment that is only half done will not count. Five of her 23 students have turned in no more than one homework assignment per week since the start of the school year. She can measure this using *permanent product* information, or the grades in her grade book (Table 8.3).

Step 2: Gather Information

What do you need to know about the students who are not turning in assignments? What needs might they have that are not being met at home or in school? How can you find out what these needs are? List several sources of information:

Mary and Angela discuss the types of assignments and the characteristics of students who are not turning in homework. They decide that the assignments are appropriate since they require only skills that the students have mastered and are in familiar formats. In looking at the students, they see that none of their parents have been able to come to parent conferences this year.

Mary talks with the students, discovering that they have no dedicated space or time at home for homework and that their parents are too busy to help them. Previous teachers note that they were not in the habit of turning in homework in second grade. Mary hopes that she can change this pattern.

Step 3: Determine What Is Maintaining the Problem Behavior

What consequences usually cause students to turn in homework? Why are these consequences not working for the students in this scenario? What can be done about it?

There are several consequences related to missing homework assignments that should be causing these students to do their homework. Their grades are lower, Mary scolds them for neglecting their work, and they have even received negative comments from their classmates. So why do they keep refusing to complete homework? Clearly the consequences are not really *punishments* (Table 8.2) since they are not causing the behavior to change.

Mary decides to look at the situation from the other side and discuss what would motivate these students to do their homework. She realizes that, to be successful in this, they would have to independently locate the necessary space, materials, and solitude at home; complete the work; and then put it in a safe place and remember to bring it to school. Their task is a much different one than that of a student who comes home to a parent who asks about homework, provides materials, assists with completion, and facilitates packing it up to be returned. The five students need both physical support and a strong motivator to change into students who do homework.

Step 4: Develop a Plan

Think about your suggestions for increasing behavior and apply them to Mary's situation. What plan would you develop that has both physical support and a strong motivator?

Once these two requirements have been identified, working out a plan is relatively easy. To address the first need, Mary decides to set up special homework folders for these students. With some of her PTA money she will purchase colorful portfolios, pencils, sharpeners, and markers. She will set these up in an organized way and staple a schedule inside the front cover. The schedule is a place for them to write their assignments and check off when they are complete. She hopes that this will help with organization, materials, and bringing assignments to school.

The second factor is also just as important, though. The students need to have a strong reason to make the effort to use these new materials, some sort of *positive reinforcement* (see Table 8.2). While external rewards such as candy might make a difference, Mary is uncomfortable with this idea, so she comes up with a plan that uses social rewards. Every morning, Mary's students will meet in "homework groups." In these groups, they will check each other's homework and fill in a graph showing the number of students who completed homework in the group.

Each graph will be posted, and the groups that achieved 100% will be praised. Mary believes that if the students are accountable to the classmates in their group, they will be more likely to put in the effort necessary to complete the assignments. She knows that there will be problems, such as incomplete homework and students who do not change their habits, and she discusses possible actions she can take in these situations with Angela.

Step 5: Implement the Plan

What do you think of Mary's plan? What are the most difficult aspects? What are the strengths? What other rewards could work for these students?

Mary purchases the portfolios, organizes them, and gives them to the students in individual meetings. She talks to each of the five students about how to use the portfolio and materials and promises that she will help them be sure that their assignment is written on the schedule daily. They seem excited and promise to start doing their homework.

She then sets up five homework groups, with one of the target students in each group, and develops a routine that they will follow each morning. This involves community-building activities, such as selecting a team name or playing a game, and homework-monitoring tasks, including completing the graph. She emphasizes the importance of maintaining positive and supportive interactions.

In the first week of implementation, Mary reports that the plan is working well. The students are excited to meet each morning and enjoy the activities. She has had to monitor their interactions carefully and help some groups work out a few issues, but she is generally satisfied that strong group bonds are being formed. The five students started out well, using her extra support in recording assignments and monitoring materials and bringing in completed work each day.

Step 6: Monitor the Plan

Fortunately, Mary does not let up on her close monitoring of the interactions of the groups because some problems begin to arise in the second week. Four of the groups are continuing to experience success. The target students are clearly motivated to do their work so that their group members will not be disappointed, and they are reminding her to help them stay organized. However, one student has slacked off on homework completion and is being pressured by his classmates. They are not satisfied with their graph showing only partial group completion.

Mary talks to the student, learning that his family is now living in a campground, where there is no electricity at night. She finds a way that he can complete his assignment each day in school before his bus leaves.

As the year progresses, the groups continue to function well. Mary finds that she has to keep a close watch on the group exchanges, and she is quick to intervene if negative patterns arise. She knows that these groups will not work as positive reinforcement if the students do not feel good about working together. But the students grow to be very supportive and caring toward each other, and she hears them reminding their friends to be sure to get assignments completed. The graphs are a continuing source of motivation, and Mary adds a motivator by promising a special "games hour" for each week in which all the groups show 100% completion. She is very pleased with the results of her behavior plan and knows that she has a new tool, a process that works well in addressing difficult situations that she may encounter as a teacher.

Behavior is communication. Functional behavioral assessments (FBAs) and behavioral intervention plans (BIPs) are required to be developed for students with disabilities in certain situations, but they are also an effective way to change the behavior of all students (Zirpoli, 2008). They are based on the behavioral approach to student motivation, as they examine and manipulate factors that are maintaining student actions.

One belief related to this approach is that behavior serves as a form of communication, even for people who have good verbal skills. The systematic FBA and BIP program leads you through the steps that determine what the difficult behavior is actually communicating. Then the student can be taught more appropriate replacement behaviors that will communicate the same information. Systematic methods such as *differential reinforcement of lower rates of behavior* and *differential reinforcement of other behaviors* are used to decrease the unacceptable behavior, and *positive reinforcement* increases the new behavior that serves the same function (see Table 8.2).

When students struggle, we encourage them to keep trying. Persistence has been shown to be one of the components of success, so we tell them to keep working on tasks that are very difficult for them. We know that, with persistence, they will succeed. We, too, must be persistent in working on student behavior that is difficult. Students who have significant behavior issues need to know that teachers will not give up on them and will not decide that they are too disruptive or different. With persistence and the use of a systematic plan, we can succeed.

SCENARIO 3

Tony is concerned about David, who is in a ninth-grade history class. David is usually well behaved, but about twice a week he seems to blow up. He does things like slam his book down, talk loudly about how much he hates history, and act generally disruptive. It often gets so bad that Tony has to send him to the office for the rest of the period. He wonders if another student is setting David off, but the students seem as mystified as he is about the reason for

Table 8.5. Developing a behavior plan

	Action	David's Plan
Step 1	Define the problem behavior	
Step 2	Gather information about the behavior	
Step 3	Determine what is maintaining the behavior	
Step 4	Develop a plan	
Step 5	Implement the plan	
Step 6	Monitor the plan	

David's outbursts. After looking at David's records, Tony finds that he had difficulty learning to read in elementary school and has always been embarrassed about his oral reading ability. Tony also realizes that David seems to blow up on the days that students are asked to read aloud. Develop a behavior plan for David using the steps in Table 8.5.

Some resources that can help you with behavior plans include the following:

Functional behavioral assessment: http://maxweber.hunter.cuny.edu/pub/eres/EDSPC715_MCINTYRE/FBA.html
Center for Effective Collaboration and Practice: http://cecp.air.org/fba
Examples of plans: http://www.advocatesforspecialkids.org/pb_plan_samples_templates.htm

SUMMARY

- Special needs can relate to academic, behavioral, or social areas.
- When a student or group of students does not respond to the system of consequences that is present in most good classrooms, a behavior plan may be necessary.

- A behavior plan can apply to an entire classroom, a small group, or an individual student.
- A behavior plan is developed through six steps:

  Step 1: Define the problem behavior
  Step 2: Gather information about the behavior
  Step 3: Determine what is maintaining the problem behavior
  Step 4: Develop a plan
  Step 5: Implement the plan
  Step 6: Monitor the plan

- In certain situations, functional behavioral assessments and behavioral intervention plans are required. Both can be effective ways to change the behavior of all students.

ON YOUR OWN

What type of special needs will you experience in the classroom? How will you differ your management approach to address the specific need of the student?

FURTHER READING

Elementary Focus

Friend, M., & Bursuck, W. D. (2002) *Including students with special needs: A practical guide for classroom teachers.* Boston: Allyn & Bacon.

Henley, M., Ramsey, R. S., & Algozzine, R. F. (2002). *Characteristics of and strategies for teaching students with mild disabilities* (4th ed.). Boston: Allyn & Bacon.

Kerr, M., & Nelson, C. M. (2006). *Strategies for addressing behavior problems in the classroom* (4th ed.). Upper Saddle River, NJ: Pearson/Prentice Hall.

O'Connor, R. E., & Jenkins. J. R. (1996). Cooperative learning as an inclusion strategy: A closer look. *Exceptionality, 6*(1), 9–51.

Sapon-Shevin, M. (1999). *Because we can change the world: A practical guide to building cooperative, inclusive classroom communities.* Boston: Allyn & Bacon.

Soodak, L. C., & McCarthy, M. R. (2006) Classroom management in inclusive settings. In C. M. Evertson & C. S Weinstein (Eds.), *Handbook of classroom management: Research, practice, and contemporary issues* (pp. 461–489). Mahwah, NJ: Lawrence Erlbaum Associates.

Secondary Focus

Children's Defense Fund. (2001). *The state of America's children yearbook 2001.* Washington, DC: Author.

Mastropieri, M. A., & Scruggs, T. E. (2001). Promoting inclusion in secondary classrooms. *Learning Disability Quarterly, 24,* 265–274.

Robinson, S., & Ricord Griesemer, S. M. (2006). Helping individual students with problem behavior. In C. M. Evertson & C. S. Weinstein (Eds.), *Handbook of classroom management: Research, practice, and contemporary issues* (pp. 787–801). Mahwah, NJ: Lawrence Erlbaum Associates.

Scholozmann, S. C. (2001). Too sad to learn? *Educational Leadership, 59*(1), 80–81.

Snell, M. E., & Janney, R. (2000). *Social relationships and peer support.* Baltimore: Paul H. Brookes.

Vaughn, S., Bos, C. S., & Schumm, J. S. (2003). *Teaching exceptional, diverse, and at-risk students in the general education classroom.* Boston: Allyn & Bacon.

Part Three

INTO ACTION

We spend too much of our time worrying about the mosquitoes and not enough time concerning ourselves about the health of the pond.

—Anonymous

The environment that you establish in the classroom influences all aspects of the students' learning. You are responsible to develop and maintain the structure that meets their physiological and psychological needs.

Facilitate this learning climate by establishing clear and consistent goals that are taught, modeled, and practiced. Lead your students to success by developing a classroom learning situation that meets their needs.

A boss drives. A leader leads.
A boss relies on authority. A leader relies on cooperation.
A boss says "I." A leader says "We."
A boss creates fear. A leader creates confidence.
A boss knows how. A leader shows how.
A boss creates resentment. A leader breeds enthusiasm.
A box fixes blame. A leader fixes mistakes.
A boss makes work drudgery.
A leader makes work interesting. (Glasser, 1992, p. xi)

Chapter Nine

Conclusion

Throughout this text, you have been introduced to the concept of managing your classroom by meeting the basic needs of your students. Since changes in behavior come about as a result of learning, you first identified your own beliefs about how students learn by looking at behavioral, cognitive, affective, social, and ecological theories. Your thinking regarding how a student learns guides you in the development of a management philosophy and ultimately a management plan.

You then explored William Glasser's teachings regarding the five basic needs and how meeting these needs establishes a classroom that promotes student success. Using the basic needs as a framework, areas germane to managing the classroom environment were discussed.

At the very basic level, students need to have their physiological needs met. If a student is hungry, tired, or fearful, they are unable to stay focused in the classroom. Chapter 3 briefly mentioned the current beliefs in the nutritional needs of learners and the attempt that schools make to address those needs. The chapter also looked at the relationship between learning and homelessness.

Although you will have limited effect on a student's nutritional habits and living conditions, you can have a dramatic and immediate impact in the area of safety, both physical and emotional. Physical safety is possible through the establishment of clearly explained and modeled rules and procedures. Emotional safety is established though positive interactions with classmates and with you.

Part of this emotional security is also connected to the student's feeling of belonging. You have the responsibility to establish a safe and nurturing environment for your students. The use of cooperative groups and class meetings assist establishing congeniality and the feeling of community. Consistency and fairness are the cornerstones to this development.

How boring and dull life would be if there were no fun or humor. The classroom is no different. Chapter 5 explored ways to bring enjoyment into the classroom. If you can make learning fun and enjoyable for your students, they in turn will be more engaged in the learning process. And the reverse it true: if students are engaged in the learning process, school is more fun and enjoyable.

As children grow older and mature, freedom becomes more important to them. By allowing students to make choices, you are using their need and desire for freedom to promote learning. Offering choices in academics and behavior helps students accept the responsibility for their actions and holds them accountable for their learning.

Power, the subject of chapter 7, is the final basic need discussed. Power is addressed through both your power and student power. You gain power in the classroom through practicing effective communication skills. How you communicate with parents and students plays a big role in how well your classroom is managed. Also discussed in chapter 7 was the power students gain from their own success. You can assist students achieve mastery through developing a positive classroom climate and providing instruction that ensures success.

Chapter 8 dealt with meeting the special needs of students. In this chapter, you looked at specific ways to track and modify disruptive behaviors. The data collection in classroom management is a vital component that can validate practices or identify areas of need.

It is now time to put the learning into a plan. Using the plan framework provided, begin to develop a management plan that will work for you and your students.

CLASSROOM MANAGEMENT AND DISCIPLINE PLAN

Philosophy of Classroom Management

Rules

1.
2.
3.
4.
5.

Where will the rules be posted?

How will the rules be taught?

How will the rules be reinforced?

How will you involve students in the development of the rules? Parents/caregivers?

What routines and procedures will you have in place?

Describe interventions you will use to help individual students get back on track with their classroom behavior.

Describe the consequences if the student does not choose the appropriate behavior.

Describe a token/reward system you could use for the whole class.

Management plan websites include the following:

http://www.geom.uiuc.edu/~dwiggins/plan.html
http://schoolmarm.org/main/index.php?page=cmp

http://www.adprima.com/managing.htm
http://www.theteachersguide.com/ClassManagement.htm
http://www.education-world.com/preservice/learning/management.shtml
http://www.teachnet.com/how-to/manage
http://www.proteacher.com/030000.shtml

Chapter Ten

Situation Analysis

Unfortunately, each of the following cases are based on factual classroom happenings.

Read each of the situations. For each, analyze what is going on in the classroom. What are the teacher actions? What are the student actions? What is/are the problems?

After you have thoroughly evaluated the scenario, offer recommendations to help correct the problem(s). Finally, provide suggestions for preventive measures that could have been used to prevent this type of situation (Table 10.1).

Table 10.1. Case analysis chart

Analyze	Correct	Prevent

BOOK TUG

Ms. Fraizer worked hard during the first weeks of school to establish a safe and nourishing climate for her group of first graders. She implemented class meetings as a way to bring up issues and concerns. Her students seemed to get along well. They were polite and usually followed the clearly defined rules and class procedures that they had helped define.

Each student understood that when they completed a seatwork activity, they were to select a book to read silently at their desk.

Ms. Fraizer noticed that both Pam and Michelle had completed their work and were heading toward the class library to find something to read. Both girls reach for the Amelia Bedelia book at the same time, and a tugging match with angry words ensued.

Ms. Fraizer calmly got up from her desk and took the book from the girls and put it on her desk with the statement, "Now, neither of you will have the book." Michelle immediately stomped her foot and in a whiney voice announced that there was nothing good to read and that Ms. Fraizer wasn't fair. Both unhappy girls gave the teacher a surly look before they stomped back to their desks. Pam began to draw on her desk, and Michelle started talking to the boy who sat next to her.

CLEAR YOUR DESK

The closer it got to winter break, the more out of control the students seemed to become. Ms. Pursall was at her wit's end to come up with a reward and punishment plan that would work for the students and maintain some type of control until break. Even though this was her second year teaching, she felt less prepared this year than the previous year.

Steven was by far the most out of control. Having been retained in third grade, he was now much bigger than the other seventh-grade students. Lately, he seemed more moody and in constant need of attention. Ms. Pursall felt that she had a good rapport with Steven since they were able to talk and even joke around on occasion.

This particular day, Steven seemed to come to school looking for a fight. He was angry and was even seen bullying the smaller boys. While the teacher was at the back of the class working with another student, he deliberately broke the point of his pencil and managed to kick or hit every student on the way to the pencil sharpener. Ms. Pursall suggested that he return to his seat at once. Steven replied in a rather haughty and unpleasant voice that he would return to his seat when he was ready.

This was the last straw for Ms. Pursall. She angrily told Steven that he needed to "grow up." In a fit of rage, Steven turned quickly around and, using one arm and one swoop, managed to clear everything off of the teacher's desk.

Shaken by the act of violence toward her personal space, Ms. Pursall quickly headed to the office to get someone to remove Steven from the room.

POKEMON PLUNDER

As Mr. Gray begins his third-grade math lesson, he notices that Nick has his Pokemon cards in his lap. Mr. Gray has already asked him once to put them away. When Nick notices that the teacher is looking at him, he quickly shoves the cards in his desk.

Infuriated, Mr. Gray reaches in the desk, takes the cards, and puts them in the top drawer of his own desk. He tells Nick that his parents can come and collect his cards but that the cards will not be returned to him directly.

After school, while sitting at his desk grading papers, Mr. Gray reaches in his top drawer for a red pen. He realizes that the Pokemon cards are missing. Furiously, he marches to the office and calls Nick's mother, explaining the entire situation and demanding a conference with both parents the next morning before school.

The following morning, Nick's irate parents and Nick show up at the classroom door. It seems that Nick does not know what happened to the cards. The last time Nick saw the cards, Mr. Gray was putting them in his top drawer.

RULES, RULES, AND MORE RULES

It is the beginning of Mr. Ware's second year of teaching fourth grade, and he feels more confident than he did last year at this time. It is the opening parent night, and he wants to give the impression that he is knowledgeable about teaching and pedagogy. He wants to make sure the parents understand who is in control of the classroom.

As the parents sit in the student desks, Mr. Ware sits behind his desk at the back of the room and goes over the information he has posted on the board. In a strong, no-nonsense voice, he tells them about the fourth-grade curriculum and what they can expect to see as assignments for the year.

Each day of the week is dedicated to specific homework assignments. Tests will be given on Wednesdays and Thursdays. Homework will be given every evening, and it should take the student approximately 1½ to 2 hours to complete the night's assignments. This time includes the half hour of reading aloud to a parent each evening. Monday, Tuesday, and Thursday nights will be dedicated to math, social studies, and grammar/spelling assignments. Weekend homework will be given only when necessary or in the case of special projects.

He outlines the 15 rules of good discipline that he has developed and the specific consequences for each time a rule is broken. The first time a rule is broken, a parent is called. The second time a rule is broken, the parent must come in for a conference. The third time a rule is broken, there will be a 1-hour detention.

Mr. Ware closes his presentation with a request that parents sign the document that outlines everything he just went over. Their signature indicates that they understand and support his ideas.

SEEING BLOOD

Mrs. Newell has already told her fifth-grade class that unless they see blood, their own or someone else's, they are not to interrupt her when she is with a reading group. Even as they know this, Sharmaine is standing at Mrs. Newell's side at the reading group circle shifting from one foot to the other and requesting that she be excused. Mrs. Newell knows that Sharmaine has not completed the worksheet that she has been assigned and therefore only acknowledges Sharmaine with a "no" shake of her head and a wave of her hand.

Sharmaine continues to stand at the reading circle, shifting and bouncing with her legs crossed. Mrs. Newell angrily stops the round-robin reading activity to explain to Sharmaine that she knows the rules and must return to her seat immediately.

Sharmaine quickly turns away and rushes from the room. On Sharmaine's return, Mrs. Newell immediately sends her to the principal's office.

SIMPLE MACHINES

It was the second week in December, and Mr. Exum's fourth-grade students had been working on science projects dealing with simple machines. They had worked in their heterogeneous groups to develop the machines and test their effectiveness in different situations.

Although he had never used cooperative groups before, he had recently attended a workshop about grouping and was anxious to see how his implementation had worked. During the initial instructions for the activity, Mr. Exum had assigned the jobs of record keeper, passage locator, thinking monitor, and reporter. He had even given them a description of their duties in that job.

As he walked around the class, Mr. Exum realized that students were not on task. Some students were testing the machines by trying to bounce them off the wall. One group tried to pick up a desk with their simple machine. They seemed to understand the directions and purpose of the activity but were unable to follow through with the assignment.

Mr. Exum became very frustrated with the class and demanded that they put the materials away and start on the math worksheet. He decided that cooperative learning was not effective in his classroom.

THAT'S NOT FUNNY

Ms. Amad consistently modeled and reinforced the rules that her third-grade class developed at the beginning of the year. She worked to demonstrate effective communication skills that would assist her students in expressing their wants and needs while at the same time effectively setting boundaries with their peers. Since her group of students came from very diverse backgrounds, she felt that the development of these skills was vital.

One day during lunch, Ms. Amad noticed a great deal of disturbance at the end of the boys' lunch table. Voices were raised, and it seemed a fight would break out at any minute. She quickly moved to intervene and stop the ruckus before it escalated.

What she found out disturbed her. It seemed that Eddie told a joke that made derogatory reference to several minorities who were sitting at the table with him. Instead of thinking the joke was funny, they took offense to his remarks.

The next morning, as Ms. Amad entered the school building, the principal greeted her at the door and asked her to step into the office. Several parents of the boys sitting at the table with Eddie had called and complained about the joke telling. The parents demanded to know what was going to be done about it.

WRONG FINGER

George is the class clown. He is less mature than the other eighth-grade students and is constantly trying to get attention from his classmates and the teacher. He constantly mumbles when Ms. Child is trying to give a lesson. Whenever she stops for a minute, George takes it on himself to fill in the time with comments. To the amusement and joy of the other class members, he seems to take special joy in acting out what Ms. Child is saying.

As Ms. Child stands in front of the class giving the notes on government and democracy, she notices that again George is in the back of the room acting out. This time he is pretending to give a speech regarding liberty and death. After giving him a harsh reprimand, Ms. Child turns back to the board to write an additional vocabulary term for the students to write down and look up in the back of their book. The rest of the class begins to giggle and say "aaaahhhhhh." It seems that when Ms. Child turned around to the board, George stuck up his middle finger.

References

Alberto, P. A., & Troutman, A.C. (2006). *Applied behavior analysis for teachers* (7th ed.). Upper Saddle River, NJ: Pearson/Prentice Hall.

American School Food Service Association. (1989). Impact of hunger and malnutrition on student achievement. *School Food Service Researcher Review, 13*(1), 17–21.

Bandura, A. (1977). *Social learning theory.* Englewood Cliffs, NJ: Prentice Hall.

Bandura, A. (1986). *Social foundations of thought and action.* Englewood Cliffs, NJ: Prentice Hall.

Bateman, B., & Golly, A. (2003). *Why Johnny doesn't behave.* Verona, WI: IEP Resources.

Bronfenbrenner, U. (1997). The ecology of developmental processes. In R. M. Lerner (Ed.), *Handbook of child psychology: Vol. 1. Theoretical models of human development* (pp. 993–1027). New York: Wiley.

Canter, L. (1989). Assertive discipline: More than names on the board and marbles in a jar. *Phi Delta Kappan, 71,* 57–81.

Cornett, C. (2001). Learning through laughter—again. *Phi Delta Kappa Fastbacks, 487,* 7–52.

Curwin, R., & Mendler, A. (1988). *Discipline with dignity.* Alexandria, VA: Association for Supervision and Curriculum Development.

Elias, M. J., Zins, J. E., Weissberg, R. P., Frey, K. S., Greenberg, M. T., Hayes, N. M., et al. (1997). *Promoting social and emotional learning: Guidelines for educators.* Alexandria, VA: Association for Supervision and Curriculum Development.

Ginott, H. (1972). *Teacher and child.* New York: Macmillan.

Glasser, W. (1986). *Control theory in the classroom.* New York: Harper & Row.

Glasser, W. (1992). *The quality school: Managing students without coercion.* New York: HarperCollins.

Glasser, W. (1993). *The quality school teacher.* New York: HarperCollins.

Glasser, W. (1999). *Choice Theory.* New York: Harper.

Gordon, T. (1974). *T.E.T.—Teacher effectiveness training.* New York: Peter H. Wyden.

Hitchcock, J. A. (2007). Cyberbullies, online predators, and what to do about them. *MultiMedia & Internet @ schools, 14*(3), 13–15.

Ingersoll, R. M., & Smith, T. M. (2003). The wrong solution to the teacher shortage. *Educational Leadership, 60*(8), 30–33.

Jones, F. H. (1987). *Positive classroom discipline.* New York: McGraw-Hill.

Kohn, A. (1993). *Punished by rewards.* Boston: Houghton Mifflin.

Kohn, A. (1996). *Beyond discipline: From compliance to community.* Alexandria, VA: Association for Supervision and Curriculum Development.

Kounin, J. (1970). *Discipline and group management in classrooms.* New York: Holt, Rinehart and Winston.

Landrum, T. J., & Kauffman, J. M. (2006). Behavioral approaches to classroom management. In C. M. Evertson & C. S. Weinstein (Eds.), *Handbook of classroom management: Research, practice and contemporary issues.* Mahwah, NJ: Lawrence Erlbaum Associates.

Mallot, R. W. (2008). *Principles of behavior* (6th ed.). Upper Saddle River, NJ: Pearson/Prentice Hall.

McGoey, K. E., & DePaul, G. J. (2000). Token reinforcement and response cost procedures: Reducing disruptive behavior of children with attention-deficit/hyperactivity disorder. *School Psychology Quarterly, 15,* 330–343.

Marzano, R. J., Marzano, J., & Pickering, D. (2003). *Classroom management that works.* Alexandria, VA: Association of Supervision and Curriculum Development.

Marzano, R. J. (2003). *What works in schools.* Alexandria, VA: Association for Supervision and Curriculum Development.

Marzano, R. J., Pickering, D. J., & Pollock, J. E. (2001). *Classroom instruction that works.* Alexandria, VA: Association of Supervision and Curriculum Development.

MSNBC. (2005). http://www.msnbcv.msn.com/id/16564208. Retrieved February 20, 2008.

Nelson, J. (1996). *Positive discipline* (Rev. ed.). New York: Ballantine Books.

Norris, J. (2003). Looking at classroom management through a social and emotional learning lens. *Theory Into Practice, 42*(4), 313–318.

Oliver, R. M., & Reschly, D. J. (2007). *Effective classroom management: Teacher preparation and professional development.* Washington, DC: National Comprehensive Center for Teacher Quality.

Pollock, J. E. (2007). *Improving student learning one teacher at a time.* Alexandria, VA: Association of Supervision and Curriculum Development.

Shukla-Mehta, S., et al. (2003). Twelve practical strategies to prevent behavioral escalation in classroom settings. *Preventing School Failure, 47*(4), 156–161.

Turnbull, A., Edmonson, H., Griggs, P., Wickham, S., Sailor, W., Freeman, R., et al. (2002). A blueprint for schoolwide positive behavior support: Implementation of three components. *Exceptional Children, 68,* 377–402. Available: http://vnweb.hwwilsonweb.com.ezproxy.umw.edu:2048/hww/results/getResults.jhtml?_DARGS=/hww/results/results_common.jhtml.7#record_3

Woolfolk, A. (2008). *Education psychology* (10th ed.). Boston: Allyn & Bacon.

Zirpoli, T. J. (2008). *Behavior management: Applications for teachers* (5th ed.). Upper Saddle River, NJ: Pearson/Prentice Hall.

About the Author

Suzanne Houff has worked on both an elementary and a middle school level as a classroom teacher and as a library media specialist. After completing her doctorate from Old Dominion University, she moved into higher education and now instructs preservices teachers as they work toward initial licensure and a master's degree in education.